Date Due

JUL 9 1982		SEP 2 1 1983	
JUL 2 3 1982			OCT 1 1 1983
AUG 1 9 1983		JAN 7 1984	
AUG 1 9 1983		JAN 2 9 1984	
OCT 1 2 1983		JUN 2 3 1984	
NOV 2 5 1983		SEP 4 1984	
SEP 1 2 1984	DEC 1 7 1984		
NOV 0 7 1984		JUN 6 1985	
		APR 9 1986	
		MAY 8 1986	
PRINTED IN U.S.A.	CAT. NO. 24 161	JAN 2 6 1987	

BASEBALL'S 10 GREATEST TEAMS

Other books by Donald Honig:

Fiction

Sidewalk Caesar
Walk Like a Man
Divide the Night
No Song to Sing
Judgment Night
The Love Thief
The Severith Style
Illusions
I Should Have Sold Petunias
The Last Great Season
Marching Home

Non-Fiction

Baseball When the Grass Was Real
Baseball Between the Lines
The Man in the Dugout
The October Heroes
The Image of Their Greatness
   (with Lawrence Ritter)
The 100 Greatest Baseball Players of All Time
   (with Lawrence Ritter)
The Brooklyn Dodgers: A Pictorial Tribute
The New York Yankees: An Illustrated History
Baseball's 10 Greatest Teams

Editor

Blue and Gray: Great Writings of the Civil War
The Short Stories of Stephen Crane

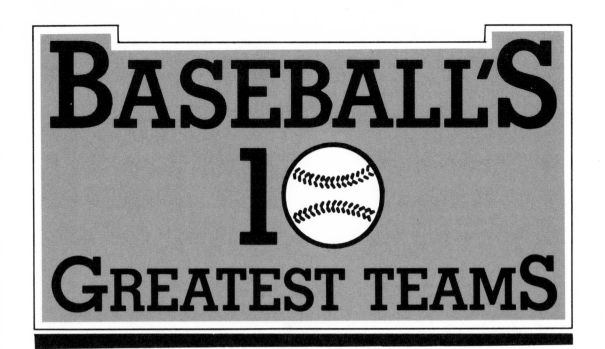

BASEBALL'S 1⚾ GREATEST TEAMS

BY
DONALD HONIG

MACMILLAN PUBLISHING CO., INC. • NEW YORK

Macmillan Publishing Co., Inc.
866 Third Avenue, New York, N.Y. 10022
Collier Macmillan Canada, Inc.

Library of Congress Cataloging in Publication Data
Honig, Donald.
    Baseball's 10 greatest teams.
    Includes index.
    1. Baseball clubs—United States—History.
I. Title II. Title: Baseball's ten greatest teams.
GV875.A1H66   796.357'0973   81-23617
ISBN 0-02-553570-6   AACR2

10 9 8 7 6 5 4 3 2 1

Printed in the United States of America

For Stanley and Peggy Honig

CONTENTS

ACKNOWLEDGMENTS

For assistance in photo research, the author would like to express his appreciation and gratitude to The National Baseball Museum and Library, and in particular to the knowledgeable and always helpful Jack Redding. Also, the Card Memorabilia Associates, Ltd., of Amawalk, New York, with a special thanks to Michael P. Aronstein for his spirited and enthusiastic help. Thanks, too, to the following for their help: Don Harrison of the Waterbury Record-American of Waterbury, Conn.; Tim Hamilton of the New York Mets publicity office; Dave Szen of the New York Yankees publicity office; Roger Ruhl, Director of Marketing for the Cincinnati Reds; Ron Modra, J. J. Donnelly, and Nancy Hogue, ace photographers; and a special word of thanks to those big league ballplayers, past and present, whose advice was helpful and who allowed the author to use photographs from their personal albums. A final word of appreciation to the following for their advice and guidance: Stanley Honig, Lawrence Ritter, David Markson, Red Smith, Allan Grotheer, Louis Kiefer, Thomas Brookman, Joan Raines, George Toporcer, Bobby Bragan, and Mary Lou La Chance.

INTRODUCTION

Since 1901, when the two-league system became the basic structure of major league baseball, there have been over 1300 teams. Picking the 10 best inevitably invokes the question of what criteria were used. One thinks of the standard definition of the great player—he can run, throw, field, hit, and hit with power—and then attempts its application to a unit of 25 men. Could the team hit for average and with power? How good was its defense? Its speed? Its pitching?

Other factors must also be taken into consideration. Because baseball has undergone certain crucial modifications in its history, these teams must be studied in the context of their times, and the standards and performance levels appropriate to those times must be taken into account. Merely winning is not necessarily a measure of a team's greatness. After all, two pennant winners emerge every year. What is significant is the consistency and the emphasis with which the winning is done. Nor must a team win by huge margins—the 1942 St. Louis Cardinals won the pennant by only two games—since the quality of the competition can often be an important factor in determining just how good a team is.

There are notable omissions. Perhaps the most conspicuous are the Oakland Athletics, who won everything in sight from 1972 through 1974. Three division titles, three pennants, and three world championships suggest an overpowering machine. A man-by-man breakdown of these teams, however, indicates that outside of their pitching—which was superb and largely responsible for the club's success—these Oakland teams were actually quite unremarkable. Offensively and defensively they were average. Also, the American League's West Division, which they dominated, was unusually weak in those years. Being the best in a weak division and having the strong pitching to carry them through the short championship series and then the World Series made the Oakland Athletics seem a much stronger club than in fact they actually were.

Another prominent omission, and one more difficult to make, is the 1919 Chicago White Sox, considered by many to be one of the genuinely great teams in baseball history. This club, which threw the World Series that year as well as an unknown number of games during the season, is excluded not because of their defective morality but because their history that season cannot be regarded as fully known. Exactly how good they were we will never know. In any event, ten teams were found that are considered superior; if the book had been extended by one team though, that team would be the 1919 Chicago White Sox.

John McGraw's 1904 and 1905 New York Giants also received serious consideration, as did McGraw's 1921–1924 clubs, winners of four straight pennants. This latter Giant outfit was formidable at the plate, but they had to be, in order to carry a pitching staff that had one 20-game winner in those four championship seasons. The 1934–1935 pennant-winning Detroit Tigers made up another offensive power-house, but they, too, had to carry a pitching staff that thinned out after several strong starters.

Also omitted are Casey Stengel's 1949–1953 Yankees and their astonishing five straight world championships. These were all solid teams, buttressed by strong pitching staffs, but none of these clubs was quite as good as the three other Yankee teams herein included. The 1954 Cleveland Indians won a league record 111 games, but they did it largely on the strength of a great, and deep, pitching staff that sustained an otherwise unremarkable club.

What differentiates the teams included in this book is a coming together and surging of an almost perfect balance of hitting, pitching, and defense strong enough not only to defeat but also to dominate the opposition. They were a conflagration of talents suddenly in full flame, exciting to watch, impossible to forget. The record books hold forever the evidence of their speed and their power, their spirit and élan; and an era in baseball history is defined by their names and their conquests.

BASEBALL'S 10 GREATEST TEAMS

CHAPTER 1

THE 1906 CHICAGO CUBS

They are perhaps the most misperceived of the great baseball teams, three members of the club having been immortalized in a mysteriously persuasive bit of poetry that finally got them hoisted—as a unit—into the Hall of Fame. It must have been a snappy double play indeed that in 1910 moved New York journalist Franklin P. Adams to write:

> These are the saddest of possible words—
>   "Tinker to Evers to Chance"
> Trio of Bear Cubs and fleeter than birds—
>   "Tinker to Evers to Chance"
> Ruthlessly pricking our gonfalon bubble,
> Making a Giant hit into a double,
> Words that are weighty with nothing but trouble—
>   "Tinker to Evers to Chance."

If Adams, a devoted Giant fan, had foreseen the generations of glory he was going to radiate upon his tormentors he may well have hesitated before putting pen to paper. The poem has had one rather perverse consequence, however—baseball scholars have gone to great lengths to prove that Tinker, Evers, and Chance really weren't that deadly when it came to clicking off double plays; were, in fact, not nearly as prolific as certain other infield combinations of the day. But this scholarly diligence has had little impact on the legend of Joe, Johnny, and Frank, proving that the pen is mightier not only than the sword but the bat as well.

Joe Tinker

Johnny Evers

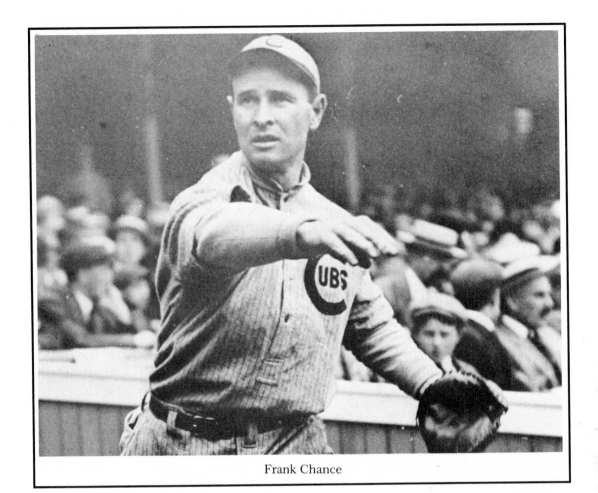
Frank Chance

Third-rate poetry and sober-faced scholars aside, Tinker, Evers, and Chance were the heart of the infield of a team that ran off 116 victories against just 36 defeats in 1906, a win total that has withstood the assaults of some powerhouse teams for more than three quarters of a century. The closest a National League team has come to the Cubs' high-flying season was 110 wins, achieved by the 1909 Pittsburgh Pirates. The 1927 New York Yankees, considered by many a thoughtful person the most formidable team of all, won a mere 110, the American League record until the 1954 Cleveland Indians put away 111 opponents.

The *Reach Official Guide* for 1907 described the 1906 Cubs thusly: "The Chicago team far outclassed any of its competitors in every department of play." They were "the best balanced team in the world," with "the best pitching corps of any club, two of the best catchers in the profession, a fast fielding and hard hitting infield and outfield, more than the average number of quick thinkers and fast base runners."

They were also, apparently, a noble group of athletes, for the *Guide* deemed it appropriate to append this observation: "It is a pleasure to add that the team played clean as well as aggressive ball, and was entirely free from public or private rows or scandals, and was in every way a credit to Chicago, the National League, and the profession." A fine accolade, making one wonder what else was going on in the game at that time to have made it necessary to state it.

It is doubtful that John J. McGraw was as delighted with the Cubs as was the *Reach Guide*. Buoyed by a pitching staff that included two of the game's most prolific winners, Christy Mathewson and Iron Man McGinnity, John J. had begun the season with every expectation of carrying off a third straight pennant. And as a matter of fact, the Giants won a creditable 96 games, enough to take many a pennant, but no cigar in that summer of 1906, for all it earned them was second place, 20 games down the road from those all but unbeatable Cubs.

The Giants kept pace with the Cubs until the end of May, the two teams seesawing between first and second place. On the 28th of May, however, the Cubs took over what proved to be permanent possession of the top spot. From that moment on they stayed in high gear. Not only did they not relinquish first place again, but they soon resembled (in the eyes of the rest of the league) an object disappearing down the wrong end of a telescope. They simply began winning and never stopped. Their pace was steady and consistent, their longest win streak being 14. If McGraw hoped they would wilt in the August heat, he was disappointed, the Cubs posting a 26–3 won-lost record in that most debilitating of baseball months.

The Cubs were a remarkable road club that year, showing a 60–15 record in between getting on and off trains, as against 56–21 while under the influence of home cooking. Nor were they one-year wonders. Fielding pretty much the same team, they also won pennants in 1907 and 1908, with a three-year record of 322 wins as against just 130 losses, a 107–43 yearly average.

The team was managed by its 29-year-old first baseman, Frank Chance. Chance, a Californian, had taken over as manager in mid-season 1905. Originally a catcher when he joined the team in 1898, he had been converted to first base in 1903 and with some hard work became one of the best at the position. A tough, smart skipper, he was a natural leader (he was called the "Peerless Leader," also "Husk," for his fine physique which included a pair of fists that were always ready to augment his point of view).

The player-manager set a good example that year, batting .319, fourth best in the league, and set an even better example as a hustler by stealing a league-leading 57 bases. Chance's verve on the bases must have been inspirational as the Cubs stole 283 bases that year, second in the league to the Giants' 288. Those dashing Cubs had seven men with 25 or more stolen bases. This speed complemented an attack that led the league in batting (.262) and hits (1316). They also led in runs, runs batted in, triples, slugging, and fielding, making by far the fewest errors in the league. Their .969 fielding average set a new major league record for defensive efficiency.

The Cubs' fielding record suggests that in spite of bad poetry and revisionist historians, that infield must have been pretty hot stuff. Tinker, a wide-ranging shortstop with a strong arm, led the league in fielding with a .944 mark. If that seems low, one must bear in mind that in this era gloves were small and skimpy and infields had the surface quality of unpaved roads. And at that time many official scorers felt that if a man got within whistling distance of a ball it should have been caught.

Second baseman Johnny Evers was the team's spark plug. Small, feisty, combative, Johnny was a nonstop chatterbox on the field, to the extent that both Chance and Tinker sometimes wished he was in the outfield. One of the game's all-time sharp thinkers, he was called "the Crab." Some say the name was bestowed for the way he moved on the diamond; others say it was for his often briny disposition. Johnny was in constant battle, with umpires, opponents, even teammates. Tinker finally tired of his partner's querulous nature and stopped talking to him, except when necessary in the heat of combat. Evers batted .255 in 1906 and stole 49 bases.

At third base for the Cubs in 1906 was a man whose name was for years featured in trivia questions: Who played third base on the Tinker to Evers to Chance infield? The answer is Harry Steinfeldt, and there was nothing trivial about his baseball abilities. This sure-handed third baseman had a powerful throwing arm. In 1906 Steinfeldt, who in the late 1890s gave up a career as a touring minstrel to go into baseball, led the Cubs with a .327 batting average, second in the league to Honus Wagner's .339. In that age of modest offensive prowess, he led the league with 176 hits and 83 runs batted in. He also topped third basemen in fielding percentage.

Behind the plate the Cubs had one of baseball's great catchers of the early days of the century, Johnny Kling. Kling, who had been with the team since 1900, possessed a strong, on-the-money throwing arm that for decades was considered the measuring rod for young power-throwing catchers. He also possessed a baseball sense that his contemporaries described as impeccable. In 1906 the 31-year-old Kling had an outstanding season with a .312 batting average. His .982 fielding mark was tops among catchers, giving the team three of the league's top gloves, along with Tinker and Steinfeldt.

Playing right field for the Cubs was Frank Schulte, known as "Wildfire." The 23-year-old Schulte, in his second full big-league season, tied for the lead in triples with 13 and batted .281. He also hit

Harry Steinfeldt

seven home runs, which seems hardly worth mentioning in light of what today's huskies can do in a week, but back in those unruffled summers it was good enough to place him fourth in the league behind Tim Jordan's 12 and Harry Lumley's 9. A few years later, in 1911, Schulte became the first big leaguer in the twentieth century to hit over 20 home runs in a season when he hit a then-impressive 21 long ones.

In left field was Jimmy Sheckard, a 10-year veteran obtained the previous December in a trade with the Brooklyn Dodgers. In 1903 the fleet, compact Sheckard had achieved the rare feat of leading the league in both home runs and stolen bases (a feat since equaled only twice, by Ty Cobb in 1909 and Chuck Klein in 1932). Jimmy was a key addition to the club, batting .262, stealing 30 bases, and giving the Cubs some superb outfield play. His .986 fielding average was second best among National League outfielders that season.

The center fielder, Jimmy Slagle, was a weak link on offense with a .239 average, but by all contemporary reports was an outstanding ball hawk with an arm baserunners preferred not to test.

The 1906 Chicago Cubs were a club of strong defensive skills and

Johnny Kling

Pat Moran, Johnny Kling's back-up man. Pat caught 61 games in 1906, batting .252. This picture was taken in the old Polo Grounds in New York.

Wildfire Schulte

Jimmy Sheckard

Solly Hofman, a handyman who filled in for the Cubs at both
infield and outfield positions in 1906. He batted .256 that year.

timely hitting, leading the league in both departments. What elevates this team to the ranks of all-time greatness, however, is the pitching staff.

In an era where pitching, generally, dominated the game, the Chicago Cubs staff was preeminent. Between 1905 and 1909 the Cub pitchers as a unit never posted an earned run average higher than 2.14, leading the league in four of those five years, and they led the league for five consecutive years in shutouts, averaging 28 a year.

With their great pitching and strong defense, the Cubs were extremely tough in low-score games, winning nine times by 1–0 scores in that memorable 1906 season. The staff hurled four one-hitters, a league record, and over the course of the season held the opposition to just 379 runs, another record for parsimony. Frank Chance's pitchers had a 1.76 earned run average that year, leading the league in that department as well as in shutouts and strikeouts.

The king of the hill for Chance was a 29-year-old right-hander with the resounding name of Mordecai Peter Centennial Brown (the Centennial was for being born in 1876). In addition to his fine array of given names, Brown had a couple of nicknames. One was "Miner," for having been reared in a coal-mining area, and the other was "Three Finger," the name that has stuck most tenaciously to him.

Brown earned his digital appellation the hard way—losing part of the index finger on his right hand to a corn shredder while a boy back home in Indiana. If any corn shredder ever belonged in the Hall of Fame, it was this one, for in redesigning young Mordecai's right index finger it enabled him to throw a baseball with a release that made the ball take a nasty dip. As a consequence, most of Brown's deliveries were rolled into the able gloves of his infielders.

Brown came to the big leagues with the Cardinals in 1903 and after that season was traded to the Cubs for right-hander Jack Taylor, a fairly good pitcher whom the Cubs reacquired midway through the 1906 season. In 1906 Brown hit full stride with the first of six straight 20 or more victory seasons, winning 26 and losing just six. He led the league with nine shutouts and what remains the lowest earned run average in National League history, 1.04, a figure that continues to blink on and off in the record books like a neon light. (Between 1906 and 1910 the highest ERA Brown had was 1.86 in 1910, which, as a future generation was wont to say, is some kind of pitching.) The stingy Brown pitched two one-hitters that year, in addition to one two-hitter and five three-hitters.

Brown's star status frequently pressed him into service on the mound against his chief rival for pitching distinction, the Giants' Christy Mathewson. Of the 24 times these two masters went to a decision against each other, Three Finger won 13.

What made the Cubs' pitching so awesome in 1906 was the staff's depth. Four men had winning percentages of .800 or better, while six were over .700. Left-hander Jack Pfiester, in his first year with the team, was 20–8 (he was the top loser on the squad). Jack, who did the headline writers a favor when he shortened his name from Pfiestenberger, was known as "Jack the Giant Killer" for his knack of being able to beat the Giants, Chicago's bitter rival through much of the century's first decade. The staff's only lefty, Jack had an earned run average of 1.56, second best on the club behind Brown.

The third big winner on the staff was Ed Reulbach, called "Big Ed" because he stood at 6'1", then a conspicuous height. Beginning in 1906, Reulbach was the National League's most difficult pitcher to beat, leading the league in winning percentage for three consecutive years, from 1906 through 1908, something no other National League pitcher has achieved and only Lefty Grove in the American League has equaled.

In 1906 Big Ed had a record of 20–4 (some record books give him 19 wins) for a percentage of .833. Completing 20 of 24 starts, he tossed six shutouts and had an ERA of 1.65. The 23-year-old right-hander, in his second year with the Cubs, put together a 12-game winning streak during the year, which was the best among those hard-to-beat Cub pitchers in 1906. In 1908 Reulbach achieved a record for one-day efficiency when he tossed a doubleheader shutout against Brooklyn, the only time this has ever been done.

Another high-percentage winner on that staff was 26-year-old Carl Lundgren. Lundgren was 17–6 for a .739 mark, with five shutouts and an earned run average of 2.21, highest on the staff.

As if they did not already have enough pitching, the Cubs swung a mid-season deal with Cincinnati for a big, 25-year-old righty with the fine name of Orval Overall. Orval showed his appreciation at being ransomed from the second division by running up a 12–3 record for the Cubs, with a 1.88 earned run average. Lest one think there is something suspicious about all of those earned run figures under two, it should be noted that only two other pitchers in the league—Pittsburgh's Vic Willis and Lefty Leifield—were able to do as well.

This was an era when relief pitching was little known, and totally unknown as a specialty. Pitchers were expected to finish what they started. The Cubs, for instance, had 125 complete games that year, impressive but still only the third best figure in the league. When trouble occurred on the mound, more times than not it was a regular starter who had to interrupt his day off to come in and try to hose down the opposition.

Another mid-season acquisition (reacquisition, actually) who finished what he started was Jack Taylor, the man originally dispatched to St. Louis for Mordecai Brown. The Cubs sent righty Fred Beebe to St. Louis after Fred had logged a 7–1 record (apparently not good

Mordecai (Three Finger) Brown

Jack Pfiester

Ed Reulbach

Carl Lundgren

Orval Overall

Jack Taylor

enough on that staff) in exchange for Taylor. Jack, who had completed 17 out of 17 for the Cardinals, was almost as thorough with the Cubs, completing 15 out of 16 and posting a 12–3 record, same as Overall's. Getting into the spirit of things, Taylor put into the books an earned run average of 1.84. There must have been something inspirational about the Chicago mound that year.

This fine, highly professional team, led by their remarkable pitchers, began in 1906 a five-year dominance of the National League, gaining four pennants and one second-place finish. Ironically, in their greatest year, 1906, when they won their record 116 games, they were upset in the World Series by their crosstown rivals, the White Sox, in what remains the only all-Chicago series. The White Sox, known as "The Hitless Wonders" for their team batting average of .230 and season's output of six home runs, should have been no match for the Cubs. Perhaps the Cubs were overconfident, or perhaps the White Sox were just one of those curious teams that has won destiny's smile (one thinks of the 1969 New York Mets). In any event, the Cub pitchers behaved with uncharacteristic generosity in that long-ago October, allowing the White Sox a little over three runs per game, just enough to make the difference.

In spite of their October stumble, however, the 1906 Chicago Cubs remain one of baseball's outstanding teams, having left behind a win total that not even teams playing in expanded schedules have approached.

CHAPTER 2

THE 1911
PHILADELPHIA ATHLETICS

Poetry and money. Poles apart, they remain among the world's constants, each capable of evoking a fascination and rendering things memorable and enduring. For instance, infields of long ago. It was a bit of poetry that preserves to this day the names of Tinker, Evers, and Chance. And it was a declared dollar value that brought lasting attention to the infield of the 1911 Philadelphia Athletics.

At first base Connie Mack had John ("Stuffy") McInnis, at second Eddie Collins, at shortstop Jack Barry, and at third base Frank ("Home Run") Baker. When Connie pridefully said he would not take $100,000 for them they became known as "The $100,000 Infield." Before there is any eyebrow raising, one must understand that that was a stupefying amount of money in those gentle and uncomplicated years. But Mc-Innis, Collins, Barry, and Baker were indeed a splendid quartet of players; in truth, one of the great infields of all time. (A few years later Connie did succumb to the lure of the long green, accepting $35,000 from the Yankees for Baker, $50,000 from the White Sox for Collins, and an undisclosed amount of loot from the Red Sox for Barry.)

Connie Mack, who originally met the world as Cornelius Mc-Gillicuddy, was born in East Brookfield, Massachusetts, in 1862, midway through the Lincoln administration; he died in 1956, during the second Eisenhower administration. Connie spent 72 of his 94 years in professional baseball, as player, as manager, and as club owner. He managed for 53 years, including a 50-year stint with the Athletics from 1901 through 1950. He no doubt knew the game, but owning the team also contributed to his job security. Owner Mack could never find it in his heart to fire manager Mack, not even after seven last-place finishes from 1915 through 1921.

History records that he was never thrown out of a game. His refusal to use profanity was no doubt a factor, as was his temperate disposition. Also, he wore street clothes and managed from the bench, limiting his opportunities for bringing umpires to a boil. To the baseball world he was the personification of dignity and integrity. To his players he was a father image and most of them maintained a deep and lasting affection for him. The harshest thing any of his employees ever had to say about "Mr. Mack" (as he was universally known) was that he was cautious with a buck, a not uncommon grumble made about employers in any profession.

Of all the teams Connie managed, it has been reported that the 1911 edition was his favorite. If true, then not a bad choice, since this was the first truly great ball club in American League history and one of the greatest ever. "It had everything," Mack said with the pride of an adoring parent. "Pitching, hitting, defense, speed, and brains." He wasn't kidding about the brain power—among the schools some of his men attended were Columbia University, Gettysburg College, Colby College, Baylor, Carlisle, and Holy Cross. According to Connie, "These boys, who knew their Greek and Latin and their algebra and geometry

Connie Mack

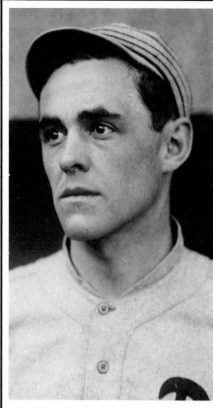

Stuffy McInnis

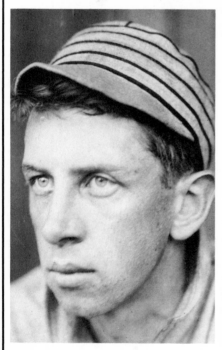

Eddie Collins

Claude Derrick, Mack's utility infielder in 1911

and trigonometry, put intelligence and scholarship into the game." Brain power is not necessarily the top line on an athlete's resumé; nevertheless, a good player with intelligence is to be preferred over one who is in danger of crushing his brains every time he sits down.

Connie's favorite team was not a squad of one-year wonders either. With pretty much the same cast of characters, this club won pennants in 1910, 1911, 1913, and 1914, plus world championships in each of those years except the last. The club batting average in 1911 was .296, which not only led the league but remained until 1920 the highest team batting mark in the twentieth century.

Much of the sock came from that highly valued infield, none of whom was over 25 years of age. At first base Mack had the 20-year-old Stuffy McInnis, whom Connie had converted from shortstop. Stuffy, a right-hander all the way, was an immediate success at the bag. According to one contemporary observer of the time, Stuffy's glovework was surpassed only "by the peerless Hal Chase," who was then and for decades after the yardstick for stopping baseballs around first base. McInnis batted .321 in 1911, his first full season, the first of eleven .300-plus years for him. His fielding got better as he went on (he led American League first basemen five times in fielding), culminating in a record-setting .999 percentage in 1921 when he made but one error in over 1,650 chances.

At second base Connie had the man who may well have been the greatest of all second basemen—Eddie Collins, nicknamed "Cocky." (Half of the distinguished $100,000 infield were known as "Stuffy" and "Cocky.") Along with his other considerable skills—Eddie could do it all—Collins had the reputation of being one of the most intelligent men ever to play big league ball. He was attending Columbia University when Mack heard about him and signed him as a shortstop in 1906. For the next twenty-five years, except for four games with Newark in 1907, Eddie was a big leaguer, a second baseman virtually all of the time, playing his last game in 1930 at the age of 43.

Collins put together one of his finest years in 1911, batting .365 and leading the league's second basemen in putouts despite missing 20 games. A lifetime .333 hitter, with a grand total of 3,310 hits and 743 stolen bases (second only to Cobb when he retired), nine times the defensive leader among American League second basemen, Collins was for a long time the automatic choice as all-time second baseman, above Nap Lajoie and Rogers Hornsby. A later generation finally succumbed to the fascination of Hornsby's batting averages and began selecting him as the number one second sacker, but those who bore witness to both men were quick to pick Eddie. And in 1911 the 24-year-old Collins was at the top of his game.

A Holy Cross product, Jack Barry, was at shortstop for Mack. The 24-year-old Barry was agile in the field and quietly effective at the plate,

Jack Barry   Frank (Home Run) Baker

batting .265 that year and stealing 30 bases. Jack, who had the second
best fielding average for American League shortstops in 1911, was one
of the steadier men at the position over the first two decades of the
century. He remained with Mack until 1915 when Connie decided to
break up his great team.

Mack's power hitter in 1911, as well as for the next few years, was
John Franklin ("Home Run") Baker. Although this Maryland strong
boy hit only 93 home runs in his 13-year career, with 12 his individual
season's high, the Home Run appellation was well applied. Actually,
Baker earned his formidable nickname that October in the World Series
against the Giants when he won back-to-back games with four-baggers
against Giant aces Rube Marquard and Christy Mathewson. That kind
of long-ball hitting would have been dramatic at any time, but in the
dead ball era it was stunning.

Baker's 11 home runs led the league in 1911, the first of four
consecutive titles for him. A man of great physical strength (he report-
edly swung a 52-ounce bat), Baker would no doubt have been a long-
baller in any era. The 25-year-old Baker's first great season was 1911
as he established himself as one of the league's premier hitters. Along

with his home run title, Frank batted .334, drove in 115 runs (second to Ty Cobb's 127), collected 198 hits, and stole 38 bases. In addition, he led American League third basemen in fielding percentage.

Another defensive leader on the 1911 A's was center fielder Rube Oldring. Oldring, a New Yorker whose square name was Reuben, fielded to a .979 average, not impressive by today's loftier standards, but good enough to be the envy of every American League outfielder that year. (A dependable glove, Rube's .978 had led the year before as well.) A right-handed hitter, the 27-year-old Oldring batted .297.

Oldring's .297 batting average made him low man among the outfield regulars. Right fielder Danny Murphy batted .329. A Philadelphia product playing for the hometown team, Danny was the veteran among the regulars. Playing his twelfth big league season, the 35-year-old Murphy had originally been Mack's regular second baseman. The arrival of Collins, however, made an outfielder of Danny. This was all right, for, as a contemporary report put it, "In the outfield Murphy shines even better than in the infield." The shining Murphy had particular radiance in his throwing arm that year, leading the league's outfielders with 34 assists, which remains one under the league record.

Left fielder Bris Lord was Connie's fifth .300 hitter among the

Rube Oldring   Danny Murphy

Bris Lord

Amos Strunk, one of Mack's reserve outfielders in 1911. The 22-year-old Strunk batted .256 that year. He became a regular the next year and played in the American League until 1924.

Topsy Hartsel, a 37-year-old veteran outfielder with Mack since 1902. He saw little action in 1911, his last year.

regulars. This gentleman, whose full name was an imposing Bristol Robotham Lord, had been acquired the year before from Cleveland and in 1911 put in his finest big league season, batting .310 and salting his 178 hits with 37 doubles.

The Athletics were particularly strong behind the plate that year. The regular catcher was 30-year-old Ira Thomas. He was an excellent receiver, highly intelligent, and along with Collins one of the field leaders of the club. Ira batted .273. There can be no better testimony to Thomas's value behind the plate than a quick look at the batting average sported by his back-up man that year. Second-string catcher Jack Lapp caught 57 games and batted .353. Despite this lusty hitting, the 26-year-old, left-handed, swinging Lapp was unable to dislodge Ira from the top job.

The team, one of Mack's masterpieces, had been put together carefully and shrewdly through trades and minor league purchases. McInnis, Barry, Collins, and Murphy had all been shifted from the positions they had originally come to the big league playing. But Mack, at the peak of his managerial genius in those early years, knew exactly what he was doing. Not only did his club lead the league in hitting, but also in fielding, committing far fewer errors than any other club.

It was during that spring of 1911 that Mack stated his philosophy of spring training: "There is no good in putting a team of ballplayers right on the edge for the opening of the season. The players should be conditioned slowly. The race is so long that, no matter how carefully the men are worked, the players individually and collectively are certain to go stale at some stage of the campaign. For this reason I do not believe in working players too hard down south. A complete rest of a day or two does them more good than harm, for when they return to the field they go at their work with more zest than if they had to do many hours exercise each day."

This perspective on conditioning was diametrically opposite that taken by John McGraw, who insisted his teams be poised at the cutting edge of readiness for the opening of the season. It was McGraw's contention that a quick getaway could have a demoralizing effect on certain teams and cost them some of their competitive spirit.

At the beginning of the season it appeared that Connie might have gone a bit too easy on his men at their Savannah, Georgia, training camp. The Athletics lost six of their first eight games and continued to stumble along. Two weeks into the season found them in last place. Meanwhile, the Detroit Tigers, led by Ty Cobb who hit .420 that season, won 20 of their first 22 games.

By April 27 the Athletics were in a three-way tie with Chicago and Boston for fourth place. On May 9 they were third. On May 24, playing a steady, efficient brand of ball now, they were second, trailing Detroit. It became a two-team race for the rest of the summer. In mid-July

Jack Lapp

Mack brought his team into Detroit for a four-game series and dropped all four. Soon after, however, the Tigers went east where they lost 13 out of 20, including 3 of 4 to the A's. The faltering Tigers slipped out of first place on August 4, replaced by the Athletics who surged ahead in high gear from then on, finishing with a 101–52 record, 13½ games ahead of Detroit.

The primary difference between the Athletics and Tigers that season was pitching. The A's had an abundance of quality pitching, more than any other team. Connie had two future Hall of Famers on his staff; but his ace was Jack Coombs, a 28-year-old right-hander out of Colby College, who had several magnificent years before suffering an arm injury in 1913. In 1910 Colby Jack was 31–9, in 1911, 28–.12. His

28 wins topped the league, bettering the efforts of such great pitchers as Walter Johnson, Smokey Joe Wood, and Ed Walsh.

A second 20-game winner was the veteran left-hander Eddie Plank. The 35-year-old Plank, winning games for Mack since 1901, was 22–8 with an earned run average of 2.10, fourth best in the league and the ninth straight year his ERA was 2.38 or less. The quiet, self-effacing, curveballing Plank was described by a contemporary as "studious" on the mound (he was one of the first pitchers to work to spots). Eddie, a graduate of Gettysburg College, led the league with six shut-outs and posted a win percentage of .733, third best in the league.

The third of Mack's great pitching triumvirate that year was Charles Albert ("Chief") Bender, a curveballing Chippewa Indian who

Paddy Livingston, third-string catcher on the
1911 Athletics

Jack Coombs

Eddie Plank

Cy Morgan   Chief Bender

had attended the Carlisle Indian School. Mack always considered
Bender, whom he called "Albert," his money pitcher. When the stakes
were high, Bender was the man most likely to go to the mound for the
Athletics. Mack's faith was not misplaced. Always a tough man to beat,
the Chief had what for him was a fairly typical year in 1911, winning
17 and losing 5 with a 2.17 ERA. A man of great personal dignity,
Bender was often greeted on the field with cries of war whoops by turn-
of-the-century fans. Occasionally he would respond by turning to the
stands, cupping his hands around his mouth and yelling back, "For-
eigners!" The Chief, along with Plank and Collins, was later voted into
the Hall of Fame.

The 1911 A's had four of the five top percentage winners among
American League pitchers. Along with Bender, Plank, and Coombs,
who were two, three, and four in percentage (behind Cleveland's Vean
Gregg), was 31-year-old veteran righty Harry Morgan, known as Cy.
Mack obtained the tough-looking Morgan from the Red Sox in 1909
and Cy gave the A's a few good years before his arm gave out in 1912.
One of those years was 1911 when he was 15–7 with a 2.70 earned run
average.

Harry Krause

Dave Danforth, a 21-year-old left-hander who was 5–2 for the A's in 1911

Ira Thomas and Connie Mack

Left-hander Harry Krause was Mack's fifth pitcher to win in double figures in 1911, racking up a 12–8 record. Krause had made a brilliant debut in 1909, the 22-year-old rookie winning 18 and losing 8 and leading the league with a sparkling 1.39 earned run average. Though arm miseries slowed him down in 1910, he came back with his fine 1911 season, but his arm went lame again the following year and what might have been an outstanding career came to a premature end.

Mack's superb team kept rolling along that October in the World Series, winning a second consecutive championship when they beat McGraw's Giants in six games. Bender, Coombs, and Plank did all the pitching, limiting the Giants to a .175 team batting average. Baker's home runs and some strong hitting by Barry and Murphy led the way for Connie's boys as they twice defeated the mighty Mathewson.

A post-season commentary on the 1911 Athletics had some pointed things to say about Mack's theory of spring training, but at the same time bore out Connie's contention about it being preparation for a long season. The article commented on Bender and Coombs having been "slow in rounding into form." There were words of praise for "the splendid fielding of the infield; superior base running and clever 'inside' work, and a steady concert of action that made the whole team appear to be working like a well-oiled piece of machinery."

The article went on to say that in winning the championship for the second consecutive time the Athletics "demonstrated superiority if ever a champion team did. This illuminating demonstration of its power was given in the face of the fact that the team started the season in poor condition due in a measure to incomplete training." It had "to work its way up from the bottom; it had to surmount the apparently unsurmountable lead of the one team that had always given the team its hardest fight. That it should win the championship again under such conditions was remarkable; but that it should also do so with ease, grace, and precision . . . is astounding and indisputably stamps the Athletic team as one of the most powerful baseball machines ever put together. In point of natural strength, vigor, ability, resourcefulness, balance, brains, power of initiation, and execution the Athletic team has no equal in the arena today."

Connie couldn't have said it any better.

CHAPTER 3

THE 1927
NEW YORK YANKEES

I n 1927 Wilbert Robinson commit-
ted what some construed as an act of heresy. He called the New York
Yankees the greatest team he had ever seen. The Brooklyn Dodgers
manager thereby put the Yankees above the team that had hitherto
been the touchstone for collective greatness, the fabled Baltimore Orioles of the 1890s, for whom Robinson had caught. Robinson's opinion
was bitterly contested by many, his old Baltimore teammate (and then
New York Giants manager) John McGraw among them.

Robbie was right, even though it was an apples and oranges kind
of comparison. The game had changed radically from the days when
McGraw and Robinson and the rest of the Orioles (they included Wee
Willie Keeler, Hughie Jennings, and Joe Kelley) slapped and bunted
and stole and hit-and-ran themselves to glory. By 1927 baseball had
become a power game and the Yankees were playing it with a ferocity
and devastation that was unprecedented.

The spread between Yankee power and that of the rest of the
league was astonishing. The New Yorkers clubbed a record 158 home
runs in 1927; their nearest competitors in long ball were the Philadelphia Athletics who hit 56. Babe Ruth soared to new heights with his
magical 60 full distance shots, meaning that Ruth by himself out-ho-
mered every American League *team* that year. He had done this once
before, in 1920, when his 54 home runs topped every team in the
league. But in 1927 he was aided and abetted in his commission of
mayhem as never before.

The '27 Yankees—it is a phrase that stands by itself in the lexicon
of baseball, connoting mountaintop greatness—set records by scoring
975 runs and posting a .489 slugging average, which is still the major

league record. They batted .307 and led the league in everything except doubles (they were second) and stolen bases. They had the individual leaders in every offensive department except stolen bases and batting average. They won a league record 110 games, played .714 ball, and came in ahead of a strong Athletic team by 19 games.

The decade of the 1920s belonged to the hitters. Both leagues had averages consistently in the .280s and .290s. The lively ball had come into play and the pitchers were apparently slow in adjusting to the change in the game's style. Of the thirteen .400 batting averages recorded in this century, seven were achieved between 1920 and 1925. In addition, there were half a dozen averages over .390. For a single team to have performed as awesomely as the 1927 Yankees did is impressive indeed.

The primary difference between the Yankees and their hard-hitting rivals of the era was power. The New Yorkers had been hitting

Babe Ruth

Babe Ruth: The mightiest swing in baseball history

home runs in record numbers since 1920, and in 1927 they outdid themselves, easily breaking their 1921 record total of 134. Essentially, the heavy thunder was concentrated in a pair of powder kegs named Ruth and Gehrig. Baseball had never seen such back-to-back sluggers, nor, despite the sweep of years, has it since. In 1961 another Yankee combine, Mantle-Maris, did out-homer their illustrious predecessors by 115–107; however, their combined batting marks averaged out to .293,

THE 1927 NEW YORK YANKEES
31

compared to Ruth-Gehrig's .365, and their combined runs batted in total was 270, compared to Ruth-Gehrig's 339. Even allowing for the game's vicissitudes, the disparities are enormous.

First there was Ruth. Then and now, the most remarkable of all baseball players. A talent of colossal proportions, with personality in equal measure. Baseball had never seen anything quite like him, nor has it since. Nor will it. He was unique, an original.

Obtained from the Boston Red Sox for around $125,000 in December 1919, Ruth became the greatest show on earth for the next fifteen years, the most magnetic drawing card in the history of sports. The Red Sox had converted him from the game's finest left-handed pitcher into an outfielder. Beginning in 1920, when he hit a titanic 54 home runs, Ruth single-handedly tore baseball apart and restructured it to fit his image. The most fortuitous event in the game's history was the almost simultaneous arrival of Babe Ruth and the lively ball.

Ruth had a fairly routine season in 1927. He batted .356, drove in 164 runs, scored 158, and posted a slugging average of .772, the ninth time in ten years he took this title. (Of the nine highest single-season slugging averages in baseball history, six belong to Ruth.) What made 1927 special for Ruth was his home run total. On the next to last day of the season he hit his 60th, breaking the record he had set in 1921. For the fourth time in nine years he had set a new major league home run record (29 in 1919, 54 in 1920, 59 in 1921).

As mighty as Ruth was in 1927, an astonishing thing was that he had a teammate, batting right behind him in the lineup, who outhit him in every department except home runs and slugging average. Eight years younger than the Babe, 24-year-old first baseman Lou Gehrig, playing his third full year, erupted suddenly from a good hitter to a great one. A New York City product who had attended Columbia University where he starred in baseball and football while studying to be an engineer, Lou was Babe's antithesis in every way—except at home plate. The shy, modest Gehrig had signed with the Yankees in 1923, put in two years with Hartford in the Eastern League, and become the team's regular first baseman in 1925, beginning a record achievement of playing in 2,130 consecutive games from June 1, 1925 to April 30, 1939.

Young Gehrig had few better years than he did in 1927. He batted .373, the first of three times he hit over .370 in his career. He hit 47 home runs, an incredible figure for the time—only Ruth had ever done better. He led the league with 52 doubles. And he set a new major league record with 175 runs batted in, topping Ruth's 1921 mark of 171. Gehrig's RBI total is even more impressive when one realizes that, batting behind Ruth, Lou came to the plate 60 times that season after Babe had cleaned the bases. In addition, Gehrig scored 149 runs, meaning some more clout came further down the lineup.

Lou Gehrig

Gehrig going up for a high one in spring training
at St. Petersburg, circa 1927

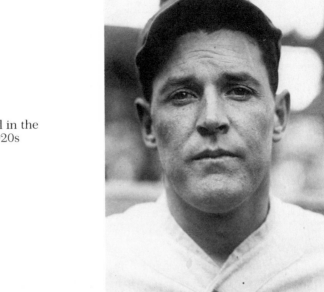

Bob Meusel in the
early 1920s

Bob Meusel scoring one of the Yankees' 975 runs in 1927

Tony Lazzeri

Ray Morehart. He filled in at second for Lazzeri when Tony had to move over to short in place of Koenig. Ray batted .256 in the big year.

Batting fifth behind the twin power plants was left fielder Bob Meusel, a 30-year-old veteran who had joined the club in 1920 after having been purchased from the Pacific Coast League. The taciturn Meusel was known as "Silent Bob." He was also known for his throwing arm, considered the most powerful in the league, a fact he demonstrated early in his career by twice leading American League outfielders in assists. Thereafter few base runners took liberties on Silent Bob.

Meusel was the third Yankee to drive in over 100 runs, bringing in 103 teammates, a strong total for a man hitting behind two sluggers who hit 107 home runs between them. Bob batted .337 that season, the highest of his career.

The fourth man on the team to drive in over 100 runs was a 23-year-old sophomore second baseman, Tony Lazzeri. One of baseball's ironies is that Lazzeri will be forever remembered as the man struck out by Grover Cleveland Alexander in their memorable confrontation in the seventh game of the 1926 World Series. On the extensive positive side of Tony's ledger, however, is the fact that he remains the greatest second baseman in Yankee history, holding down the position from 1926 through 1937.

In 1927 Tony batted .309, knocked in 102 runs (Tony had to be satisfied picking up Ruth's, Gehrig's, and Meusel's leftovers), and hit 18 home runs—third highest total in the league after Ruth and Gehrig. This, incidentally, is the only time in big league history that the top three home run spots were the exclusive claim of a single team. While Tony is enshrined as the second baseman on the '27 Yankees, he actually played only 113 games at second that year. The versatile San Franciscan filled in at shortstop in 38 games. While Tony played short, second was covered by utility man Ray Morehart who batted .256.

The fifth .300 hitter on the 1927 Yankees, their center fielder Earle Combs, a swift, handsome Kentuckian, began in 1925 a tradition of greatness for Yankee center fielders. A year after Combs' retirement in 1935 the team brought up Joe DiMaggio, and in DiMaggio's final year, 1951, young Mickey Mantle joined the team, giving the Yankees more than four decades of Hall of Fame representation in the most crucial outfield position.

Combs, who never had a bad year in the major leagues, had his greatest season in 1927. The fleet center fielder batted a career-high .356 and led the league with 231 hits and 23 triples. Combs exemplified what made the 1927 Yankees perhaps the greatest of all teams—an outstanding player having his peak or near-peak year. Ruth and Gehrig were never better than in 1927, Meusel logged his highest batting average ever, and Combs scaled his personal mountaintop with career highs in batting, hits, and triples.

Combs, batting first in the order, led off the team perfectly. Between hits and bases on balls, the sharp-eyed Kentuckian got on base

Earle Combs

Reserve outfielder Cedric
Durst. He is remembered in
Yankee history primarily for
having been traded in 1930
to the Red Sox for Red Ruffing.

When Ruth or Meusel or Combs needed some time
off—it wasn't often—Ben Paschal got a
game. He did all right, too, batting .317 when
given his chance.

Joe Dugan

Mike Gazella filled in at
third base for the ailing
Dugan. In 54 games Mike
batted .278.

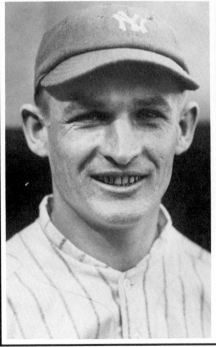

Mark Koenig

nearly 300 times. Playing lightning to the thunder behind him, he scored 137 runs. If Combs had a weakness, it was his throwing arm. Or perhaps, playing between a couple of rocket arms like Meusel and Ruth, it only seemed that way. Nevertheless, he set a standard for playing Yankee Stadium's vast center field that only DiMaggio came up to.

Combs led off; Mark Koenig, a switch-hitting 25-year-old short-stop, batted second. Purchased from the St. Paul club in 1925 for a reported $50,000, the native San Franciscan had one of his better years in 1927, batting .285, which happened to be the sixth best average on this team. Koenig was one of the few Yankees to come up with a conspicuous negative statistic that season—he led American League shortstops with 47 errors. As a matter of fact, his fielding was never the steadiest and eventually led to his being traded to Detroit in 1930.

"Jumping Joe" Dugan played third base for the 1927 Yankees. Another of the "weak links" in the batting order, Joe batted .269, a respectable figure but somewhat feeble-looking on that ball club.

Dugan was actually one of the few '27 Yankees on the down side of their careers. At 30, Joe was in his penultimate season in pinstripes. Joe had in 1917 gone straight from the campus of Holy Cross to the Philadelphia Athletics. When the A's scout, Ira Thomas, asked Joe to sign with Connie Mack's club, Joe said no. Thomas then drew five $100 bills from his pocket, showed them to the youngster and asked, "Can we get you for this?" Joe, always a blithe spirit, sized up the greenbacks and supposedly said, "For that you can get the whole family."

Mack eventually traded Dugan to the Red Sox who in turn sent him to the Yankees where Joe hit steadily in the .280s and .290s and helped the team to five pennants. His .269 batting average in 1927 was the lowest among the team's regulars.

Behind the plate the Yankees had a couple journeymen named Pat Collins and Johnny Grabowski. The 30-year-old Collins, obtained from the St. Louis Browns a few years before, did the bulk of the catching that year, holding up the mitt for 89 games. He batted .275. Grabowski, picked up from the White Sox after the 1926 season, did the rest of the catching and batted .277. Collins and Grabowski remain the most anonymous regulars (or semi-regulars) on the 1927 Yankees.

The man who manipulated this power-laden lineup was Miller Huggins. Huggins began managing the Yankees in 1918, when the New Yorkers had yet to win their first pennant. He remained as manager until his sudden death from blood poisoning at the end of the 1929 season, having won six pennants and three World Series between 1921 and 1928.

The 5'4" Huggins came to the Yankees after a somewhat undistinguished 13-year career as a second baseman with the Cincinnati Reds and St. Louis Cardinals and four years as Cardinals manager. An intel-

Pat Collins

Benny Bengough, third-string
catcher on the 1927 Yankees,
a job he held until 1930.

John Grabowski

Miller Huggins

ligent man—he gave up a career in law to go into baseball—Huggins handled men shrewdly and sensitively. In 1925 a free-wheeling, rules-breaking Babe Ruth tried his skipper's patience to the limit, and Huggins fined the game's number one attraction $5,000 and suspended him. The front office backed Huggins. When a contrite Ruth was reinstated, he no longer questioned his manager's authority and over the next few years developed a healthy respect for the man the newspapers called "The Mite Manager."

When the Yankees went to spring camp in 1927, they were favored to repeat as pennant winners; nevertheless, some question remained about their pitching. Huggins' staff was the oldest in the league. The 1926 ace, Herb Pennock, was 33 years old. The left-handed curveball artist had come to the big leagues with the Philadelphia Athletics in 1912, been traded to the Red Sox and then on to the Yankees in 1923, where he launched into the full stride of his greatness.

Huggins called Pennock "the greatest left-hander of all time." While this probably represented managerial pride speaking, Huggins, in 1927, wasn't too far wrong. In fact, the only southpaws with a clear-cut superiority over Pennock at that time would have been two of Connie Mack's old aces, Eddie Plank and Rube Waddell. Connie's current

Huggins and Ruth. After the blow-up in 1925 they gradually became friends.

Herb Pennock

Wilcy Moore

Waite Hoyt

ace, Lefty Grove, had not yet reached his peak. (The man who might well have become the greatest lefty of all time was at that moment playing right field for the Yankees.)

In 1927 Pennock, invariably described as "smooth" and "stylish" on the mound, had one of his better years, winning 19 and losing 8 for a .704 winning percentage. Not particularly fast, a control artist with a variety of breaking pitches, he looked easy to hit. "Except," said one of his opponents, "that when you swung, the ball wasn't there; or if you did hit it, it took two or three little skips right into an infielder's glove."

The ace in 1927 was 26-year-old Waite Hoyt, still trying to shake off the "Schoolboy" nickname hung on him when he left Brooklyn's Erasmus High School to become a professional ballplayer at the age of 16. Hoyt, who had come to the Yankees from the Red Sox in 1920, had his finest season in 1927, winning 22 and losing 7 and leading the league with a .759 winning percentage. His 2.64 earned run average placed him second lowest in the league.

The great surprise on the pitching staff that year was a 30-year-old freshman right-hander named Wilcy Moore. Moore was the one-year wonder on this team of fine stars. His contribution was spectacular, unexpected, and brief. He had spent 1926 pitching for Greenville in the South Atlantic League. His 30–4 won-lost record attracted the Yankees, who purchased him for less than $5,000.

The homespun, good-natured, Oklahoma dirt farmer astonished everyone by racking up a 19–7 record and the league's lowest earned run average, 2.28. Moore, who threw a sharp-sinking fastball, was primarily a relief pitcher, the first of many outstanding bullpen artists who would work for the Yankees. Years later, Waite Hoyt described Moore as the greatest one-year relief pitcher he had ever seen. And one year was pretty much what the Yankees got out of Wilcy. Whatever magic he had possessed in the Yankees' greatest season soon dissipated and the rest of his brief stay in the major leagues was undistinguished.

The fourth big winner on Huggins' staff was the 36-year-old spitballer Urban Shocker. Like Moore and Hoyt, Urban threw right-handed. He had originally joined the Yankees in 1916. A year later, in one of their rare trading mistakes, they swapped him to the St. Louis Browns, where he became one of the league's best pitchers, a four-time 20-game winner. They reacquired him after the 1924 season and he helped pitch them into the World Series in 1926 and 1927.

Shocker had a reputation for being one of the canniest pitchers in the game, superb at pitching to a batter's weakness. In 1927 he won 18 and lost 6 for a winning percentage of .750—his highest ever—and posted an earned run average of 2.84, third lowest in the league, after Moore and Hoyt. But the final call soon sounded for Urban Shocker; a year later, on September 9, he died of a heart ailment.

Huggins' pitching staff was rounded out by veteran left-hander

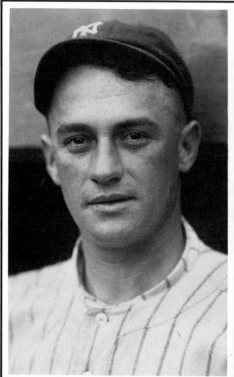

Urban Shocker

George Pipgras

Dutch Reuther

Myles Thomas, a right-handed
pitcher who was 7–4
starting and relieving

Walter ("Dutch") Ruether who was 13–6 and a strong young righty named George Pipgras with 10–3.

The reputation of the 1927 Yankees rests primarily on the club's hitting, so much so that the pitching is overlooked. They pitched, however, exceptionally. The staff's 3.20 composite earned run average stood out as the league's best, as did their 11 shutouts. The American League hit hard that year, but few dents were made on the Yankees' staff. Huggins had the league's top three pitchers in earned run average (Moore, Hoyt, Shocker), as well as five pitchers with better than .700 winning percentages (Pennock, Hoyt, Moore, Shocker, Pipgras). The '27 Yankees were only the third team in American League history (after the 1903 Red Sox and 1910 Athletics) to lead with both the highest batting average and lowest earned run average.

Legends have grown around this ball club. Perhaps the most famous concerns the day the Yankees took batting practice at Forbes Field just before the opening of the World Series against the Pittsburgh Pirates. According to the story, Ruth and Gehrig and Lazzeri and Meusel were propelling baseballs into the stratosphere with such compelling majesty that the onlooking Pirate players grew so disheartened they felt the Series was over before it started. Lloyd Waner, one of the supposed Pirate witnesses to this display, has denied it ever happened. History shows that Pittsburgh fell in four straight to the Yankees, but three of those games were tightly played, and the Yankees hit but two home runs that October, both by Ruth.

They won again in 1928 and again played the World Series in minimum time, dispatching the St. Louis Cardinals in four. Essentially the cast remained the same, but this time the magic was missing. They won 101 games, but a Philadelphia Athletics team beginning to surge up into its own years of greatness pressed them hard.

Ruth and Gehrig smoothing their bats with sandpaper

CHAPTER 4

THE 1929–1931
PHILADELPHIA ATHLETICS

B y the late 1920s Connie Mack was ready to be heard from again. After breaking up his 1910–1914 team after the 1914 World Series, Mack's Philadelphia Athletics took immediate and, it seemed, permanent possession of the American League basement. For seven consecutive years, from 1915 through 1921, the A's finished dead last, losing 100 or more games in five of those years. Attendance plummeted—the club's per game average during those seven years fell below 1,600. By the early 1920s there were some not-so-polite mutterings in Philadelphia suggesting Mack sell out and turn the fortunes of the team over to other hands. In 1924 a Philadelphia sportswriter wrote, "As long as Connie Mack is connected with the A's they'll never get anywhere."

But a year later, in 1925, Mack, who had quietly begun rebuilding his team, brought the A's in second. In 1926, spending money for new players and patiently putting the pieces in place, he finished third, just six games behind the Yankees. In 1927, with the league's attention focused on Ruth and Gehrig, Connie again placed second. In 1928, the A's threw a scare into the mighty Yankees, almost derailing the New Yorkers' run for a third straight flag, challenging them into September and finishing second again, just two and a half games out. All of the pieces were in place now as Mack prepared for an epic struggle in 1929, ready to send the mightiest of all his teams against the still formidable Yankees.

As it turned out, the Yankees were no match for the Athletics in 1929. Mack's team roared through the league with such thundering efficiency they were never threatened. By the end of May they began to run away and hide, racing toward their 104 wins and 18-game bulge over the second-place Yankees, who were just two years past having been perhaps the greatest team of all time and who still had Ruth and Gehrig and Lazzeri and Combs hitting the ball hard, abetted now by the young catcher Bill Dickey.

The Athletics were so awesome in 1929 that many people believed —still believe, for that matter—that Mack's team played better than the '27 Yankees. If the A's shone in 1929, they blazed just as bright in 1930 and 1931, the last year of their dominance. They did what Mack said a great team must—repeat. And they did so emphatically, with margins of 8 and 13½ games.

The Athletics had a solidly packed lineup during their three glory years, mostly with the same personnel. It was a set team, highlighted by four of the most dynamic talents of all time. The passage of time reduces a team, finally, to its most remarkable names. Only the loftiest peaks are still visible. Thus, for all their abundance of talent, the 1927 Yankees remain the team of Ruth and Gehrig. The 1929–1931 Athletics, however, have left behind four names that will always be synonymous with those teams, four names that will remain forever unchallenged upon the rolls of baseball greatness. Those names were the names of Grove, Cochrane, Foxx, and Simmons.

If one among them stood first among equals he was Robert Moses ("Lefty") Grove, in all likelihood the number one left-hander in baseball history, a man whose fastball could evoke shuddering memories in old opponents a half century later. What elevated Grove above the ranks of other hard throwers and places him in the rarefied company of the legendary fastballers like Walter Johnson, Bob Feller, and Sandy Koufax was his ability to throw "that thing" with remorseless, undiminishing speed for nine innings. The puckish Lefty Gomez once asked Grove what he did when trouble arose in the eighth inning of a close game. "I bear down harder," the serious-minded Grove said. "How about in the ninth inning?" Gomez asked. "In the ninth inning?" Grove said with a scowl. "Hell, in the ninth inning I just blow it by 'em." And so he did. From 1929 through 1931 Grove won 79 and lost just 15. Lest one think Lefty did it on the strength of the big bats in his lineup, it should be pointed out that he led the league in each of those years in strikeouts and earned run average.

Those were hard-hitting years in the American League. In 1929 the league batted .284, in 1930, .288, in 1931, .278. Through those three years only four earned run averages under 3.00 were recorded; three of those belonged to Grove (the other to Gomez). In 1931, when American League teams were averaging better than five runs a game, Grove's ERA was 2.06.

A dour, thin-skinned man with a volcanic temper, Grove was purchased by Mack from the independently owned Baltimore Orioles of the International League in 1924 for $100,600. In 1931 Lefty put to-

Lefty Grove

gether one of the most memorable seasons ever by a pitcher. He won 31, lost 4 and from June 8 to August 19 equaled the American League record by winning 16 straight. The streak ended on a 1–0 loss to the St. Louis Browns, the run scoring on a misplayed fly ball. After the game Lefty set another record, this one for clubhouse demolition. Those who were there remembered with awe the pitcher's virtuoso smashing of stools, shredding of uniforms, denting of lockers.

Grove's attitude toward losing was typical of this hard-bitten club. One of the purest of the mold was catcher Micky Cochrane, in 1929 a 26-year-old five-year veteran. Purchased by Mack from Portland of the Pacific Coast League after the 1924 season, the fiery Cochrane was the team's field leader. "Tough as flint," teammate Doc Cramer said admiringly of Cochrane years later. On a play at the plate, according to Cramer, it was the incoming runner who was in danger, not Cochrane. "Home plate was *his,* you see," Cramer said. "You had to take it away from him."

With Grove standing at the top of the list of baseball's left-handers (only Sandy Koufax can match him) and Cochrane frequently selected

Mickey Cochrane

Cy Perkins, fine veteran
catcher who spelled
Cochrane on the 1929 and 1930 teams

Two future Hall of Famers coming together at second base in the first game of the 1930 World Series. Cardinal second baseman Frank Frisch is applying the tag to Mickey Cochrane, who was trying to steal.

as the all-time catcher (the Yankees' Bill Dickey is the generally accepted alternative), the 1929–1931 Philadelphia Athletics possessed what was probably the most potent battery in history, with both men performing at the peak of their abilities. Cochrane's averages from 1929 through 1931 were .331, .357, and .349. No other catcher has ever posted such consistently high batting averages. In addition, Mickey led American League catchers in fielding in 1929 and 1930.

At first base the Athletics had the man called "The Right-handed Babe Ruth," James Emory Foxx. In 1929 this 21-year-old powerhouse

Jimmie Foxx holding the trophy awarded him for having been voted the American League's Most Valuable Player in 1932.

from Sudlersville, Maryland, was beginning to rip the ball with an authority equaled only by Ruth and Gehrig. In 1929 Jimmie hit 33 home runs, drove in 117 runs, and batted .354. To give some indication as to what a prodigy the muscular young Foxx was, half the teams in the American League that year hit under 50 home runs. In 1930 "Double X" hit 37 home runs and drove in 156 runs; a year later those figures were 30 and 120.

Foxx joined the Athletics as a 17-year-old pinch-hitting catcher in 1925 after having played for the Easton, Maryland, club in the Eastern Shore League. Both the A's and the Yankees were interested in the boy, but the manager of the Easton team happened to be Mack's one-time slugging third baseman, Home Run Baker. Baker, doing a favor for his old boss, saw to it that Foxx was sold to the A's.

Mack broke the youngster in gradually. By 1928 Foxx was a regular, about to break loose with the most awesome right-handed hitting the game had ever seen. He hit the ball as hard and as far as Ruth. One of his clouts against the Cardinals in the 1930 World Series flew high and far with such grandeur that one of the Cardinals' bullpen contingent said later, "We were watching that ball for two innings." Wes Ferrell, a six-time 20-game winner in the 1930s, a tempestuous sort known to breathe fire at giving up a base hit, said he was never angry when Foxx tagged him for a long one. "You just had to turn around and admire it," he said.

The fourth all-time great on Mack's 1929–1931 clubs was left-fielder Aloysius Harry Szymanski, better known as Al Simmons. This right-handed-hitting Milwaukee product joined the A's in 1924 and began notching some of the most prodigious batting averages in the league. In 1925 he batted .384, in 1927, .392. Along with Foxx, he gave the A's a duo to match the Yankees' Ruth and Gehrig. Through the three pennant-winning years Al batted .365, .381, and .390 (the latter two, league-leading figures). His RBI totals were 157, 165, and 128. In 1929 Al hit 34 home runs, in 1930 he hit 36. Outside of Ruth and Gehrig no other duo in the league could remotely compare with Foxx and Simmons when it came to hitting the long ball.

Simmons, whose unorthodox stance at the plate earned him the nickname "Bucketfoot Al," was also a super left fielder—he led the league in fielding in 1929 and 1930. His contemporaries say he had no peer for picking up balls hit down the line and throwing men out at second.

After stubbornly holding out in the spring of 1931, the tough-minded Simmons won from Connie Mack a three-year $100,000 contract, making him the game's second highest salaried player after Ruth.

Behind Grove, Cochrane, Foxx, and Simmons, Mack had an array of mere mortals who played first-rate ball. Second baseman Max Bishop was obtained from Baltimore in 1923. Max, who set several fielding

Al Simmons

Jim Moore, reserve
outfielder on the 1930–1931
pennant winners

Max Bishop

records for American League second basemen, was the club's leadoff man, an important spot on a team with the dynamite this one had in its lineup. And he was a good one. Known as "Camera Eye" for his expert judgment of the strike zone, Max consistently drew over one hundred walks a season, contributing significantly to those fat RBI totals that were accumulated behind him.

Shortstop Joe Boley was also acquired from Baltimore, for $65,000 after the 1926 season. Joe was the part-time shortstop on the 1929 and 1931 clubs, sharing the job with Jimmy Dykes in 1929 and Dib Williams in 1931. In 1930, when he played most of the year at the position, Joe led American League shortstops in fielding. Defensively, Mack's clubs were the best in the league during the three championship years, a fact sometimes overlooked. Heavy-hitting teams are not generally thought of in terms of efficient glovework; but those Athletic units led the league in fielding in 1929 and 1930 and were virtually tied for the lead in 1931.

Jimmy Dykes, who eventually succeeded Mack as manager of the A's when Connie finally stepped down in 1950, was a utility infielder in 1929, getting into 119 games and batting .327; the regular third baseman in 1930, batting .301, and again the regular third baseman in an injury-shortened season in 1931. Dykes was the club "character." A

Third baseman Sam Hale was with the Athletics from 1923 through 1929. The regular third baseman in 1929, he batted .277.

Joe Boley

Jimmie Dykes

Eric McNair, utility infielder
on the 1930–1931 teams

Dib Williams, utility infielder
on the 1930–1931 Athletics

Bing Miller

witty, mischievous man, Dykes as a rookie did not resist twitting the great Ty Cobb on occasion. On his way in from the outfield between innings, Cobb habitually stepped on second base. Frequently, when playing the A's, he would find the short, roundish Dykes standing on the base with an impish grin. "He'd snarl," Dykes recalled years later, "and call me 'hot stuff,' only he didn't say 'stuff.' "

Dykes joined the Athletics in 1918 at second base but proved versatile enough to be used at short and third. Overshadowed by the big busters around him, Jimmy did give Mack five seasons over .300.

In right field Mack had a solid .300 hitter in Edmund ("Bing") Miller. Miller was 26 years old when he came to the major leagues with the Washington Senators in 1921. A year later the right-handed hitting outfielder was traded to the Athletics, where he had the first of the nine .300 or better seasons he was to enjoy in the bigs. In 1926 he was traded to the St. Louis Browns but a year later was reacquired in a swap for pitcher Sam Gray.

Miller's batting averages in the three pennant-winning years were .335, .303, and .281. In 1930 he drove in 100 runs. A sharp-eyed singles

Mule Haas

George Earnshaw

and doubles hitter, Bing went to bat nearly 1,700 times from 1929 through 1931 and struck out just 63 times.

In center field Mack had George ("Mule") Haas, a left-handed hitting native of New Jersey who joined the club in 1928, the last piece to fall into place in the making of that all-time great team. Mule gave Connie batting averages of .313, .299, and .323. Not known for pounding the long ball, Haas belted a memorable clutch home run in the bottom of the ninth inning of the fifth and final World Series game against the Chicago Cubs. With his club trailing 2–0, he came to bat with a man on first and hit one out to tie the score. A few moments later Bing Miller drove in the winning run, giving the A's the world championship.

On the mound the great Grove teamed with hard-throwing right-hander George Earnshaw, for whom Mack paid the talent-rich Baltimore club $80,000 in 1927. In 1928 the 6'4" Earnshaw broke in with a

Right-hander Bill Shores was 11–6 in 1929 and 12–4 in 1930. A sore arm all but ended his career the next year.

Roger (Doc) Cramer

modest 7–7 season. A year later, however, he was the ace with a 24–8 record, followed by seasons of 22–13 and 21–7. The hard-throwing Earnshaw, a Swarthmore graduate, was runner-up to Grove in strike-outs in each of the pennant-winning seasons. In 1930 and 1931 he tied for the lead in shutouts. In the 1930 World Series he pitched 22 con-secutive scoreless innings against a St. Louis Cardinal team that had eight .300 hitters in the starting lineup and a team average of .314 (yes, .314). Many of the Cardinal hitters asserted that George threw harder than Grove.

"Nobody could beat us in those days," said Doc Cramer, a young outfielder on the A's in those heady years. "We'd pitch Grove, Earn-shaw, and Walberg the first three games, and we didn't care who they pitched—we had 'em wore out."

George ("Rube") Walberg, a bulky left-hander, was Mack's third ace. Rube, who joined the A's in 1923 at the age of 24, would have been the number one man on many staffs of the day, but working behind Grove and Earnshaw he had to settle for the number three spot. In 1929 he was 18–11, a year later he slipped to 13–12, but came back strong in 1931 with a 20–12 record, giving the team three 20-game winners in one season, something not even the powerful Yankee teams of the era could ever achieve.

Mack's mighty team won the World Series in 1929 and 1930, then lost to the Cardinals in seven games in 1931. What happened in the 1929 Series perhaps epitomizes exactly how powerful was the machine

Rube Walberg

It's an impromptu signing as the train bearing the Athletics
to their Florida spring training site stops at Savannah, Georgia, on
March 3, 1933. Connie Mack is lending his shoulder to George Earnshaw
as Rube Walberg looks on.

Howard Ehmke. The veteran right-hander was Mack's surprise starter in the 1929 World Series against the Cubs. Ehmke proved his manager's acumen by winning and striking out a Series-record 13 Cubs along the way. The 35-year-old Ehmke was 7–2 in 1929, his last full season in the majors.

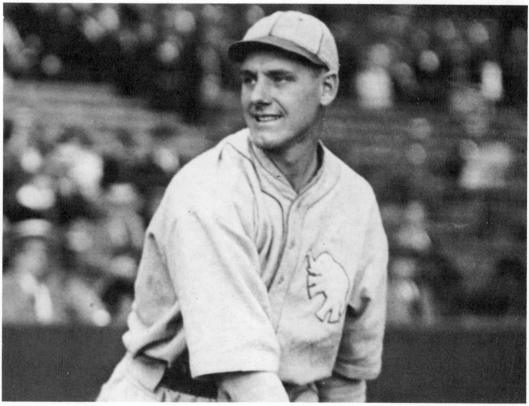

Right-hander Eddie Rommel spent his entire big league career with the Athletics, from 1920 through 1932. Overshadowed by Mack's big three in the pennant-winning years, he nevertheless posted won-lost records of 12–2, 9–4, 7–5.

Roy Mahaffey, a hard-throwing
righty, was 9–5 in 1930 and 15–4
the next year, his best
in the majors.

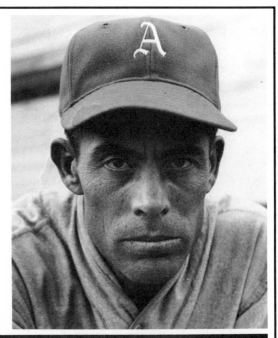

Trivia question: Who played on both the 1927 Yankees and 1931 Athletics?
The answer is this gentleman, Waite Hoyt, who joined the A's in
a mid-season deal with Detroit in 1931. Hoyt was 10–5 in his half-
season's work for Connie Mack.

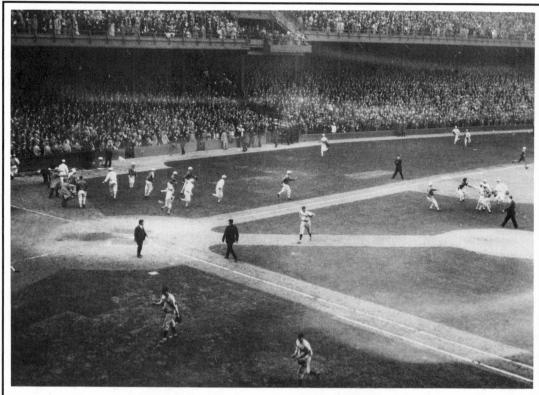

Bing Miller has just delivered the hit that gave the A's the
1929 World Series over the Cubs. The triumphant A's are heading
for Bing to give him a hero's pounding.

Mack had so shrewdly and patiently put together. Ahead two games to
one against the Cubs, the Athletics came to bat in the bottom of the
seventh inning of game four trailing 8–0. Swinging with supreme confidence—"We figured with our lineup we were never out of a game,"
Dykes said—they tore into four Chicago pitchers for the most explosive
rally in World Series history. The mayhem went as follows: Simmons
opened with a home run, Foxx singled, Miller singled, Dykes singled
for a run, Boley singled for a run, pinch-hitter George Burns popped
out, Bishop singled for a run, Haas got a three-run homer on a ball
Cubs center fielder Hack Wilson lost in the sun. It was now 8–7.
Cochrane walked, Simmons singled, Foxx singled in the tying run.
Miller was hit by a pitch, loading the bases. Dykes then doubled in the
ninth and tenth runs of the inning. The next two batters struck out. If
all of that wasn't enough for the stunned Cubs, Mack brought in Grove
to pitch the last two innings. Lefty machine-gunned his bullets, setting
down in order the six men he faced, fanning four of them.

The following day the Cubs took a 2–0 lead into the bottom of the ninth, only to see it melt under Haas's two-run homer and a rally capped by Miller's game-winning hit.

"Some team, huh?" Lefty Grove said with dour satisfaction forty-five years later.

They might have gone on, but for a combination of factors. For one thing, attendance in those great years went steadily down. Connie Mack noted that Philadelphians manifested a curious attitude toward their team in that they would turn out in greater numbers to watch their favorites battle to become champions than they would to see them defend a championship.

Mack asserted that his 1932 club was the highest-salaried baseball team in history, up to that point. Caught with expensive players and declining gate receipts, he was forced for the second time in his long career to dispose of star players for needed cash. Within a few years they were all gone—Foxx, Grove, and Bishop to the Red Sox; Dykes, Simmons, Haas, and Earnshaw to the White Sox; Cochrane to the Tigers. By 1934 Connie Mack had fallen back to the second division, there to languish for the next 14 years, remembering the 1929–1931 team, years of unmatched glory; a team so powerful and unbeatable it finally bored its fans into staying home.

CHAPTER 5

THE 1936
NEW YORK YANKEES

In 1935 Ruth was gone, club attendance was down, and the Yankees were headed for their third consecutive second-place finish under Joe McCarthy, who had won but one pennant since taking over the team in 1931. A year later, however, one of the greatest of all Yankee teams piled up a 102–51 record and won the pennant by 19½ games, setting a new major league home run record along the way with 182. They also set new standards with 995 runs batted in and for having five men drive in over 100 runs. The team compiled a .483 slugging average, one of the highest in big league history.

Nothing freakish or accidental made this team, for the 1936 Yankees launched a dynasty that would win 4 pennants and four world championships in 4 years, 7 pennants in 8 years, 22 pennants in 29 years.

It was one of the hardest-hitting seasons in American League history, the league as a whole posting a batting average of .289, saddling the pitchers with a whopping earned run average of 5.04. The Yankees' club batting average of .300 was topped by Cleveland's .304 and equaled by Detroit's .300. The New Yorkers had six .300 hitters in the lineup and seven men in double figures in home runs. Even allowing for the heavy hitting that went on in the league all year, the Yankee attack was severely punishing.

Two members of the 1927 club, Lou Gehrig and Tony Lazzeri, were still with the Yankees. Lou, who had been pounding the ball year in and year out through the decade, had another typical Gehrig year in 1936. He batted .354, drove in 152 runs, scored 167, and clouted a league-leading 49 home runs, his personal high. Going into the 1936

Lou Gehrig

Joe DiMaggio

season he had already played in over 1,600 consecutive games, shatter-ing all records, and, at the age of 32, seemed indestructible.

For years Gehrig had been laboring in the shadow of Ruth. What-ever Lou did, Babe did just a little better, or with more flair. Ruth was a titan and a Merlin; his heroics had a mesmerizing quality; they seemed more wondrous simply because they had been done by Babe Ruth. Gehrig lacked the excitement and the grandeur of his teammate. Lou hacked away day after day and year after year with brutal effi-ciency. Ruth left the Yankees after the 1934 season, leaving the shy, self-effacing Gehrig as preeminent Yankee.

In 1936, however, the team came up with a rookie who became an immediate sensation, to the extent that before the season was over his shadow was being cast further than Gehrig's. In a personality not unlike Gehrig's was embedded a dramatic flair and majesty not unlike Ruth's. Twenty-one-year-old Joe DiMaggio soon came to symbolize everything the Yankees stood for: power, class, style, and a quiet, businesslike approach to success.

Purchased from the San Francisco Seals of the Pacific Coast League for $25,000 and five minor league ballplayers, Joe stepped into the center field spot vacated by the veteran Earle Combs after the 1935 season. The youngster was perhaps the most exquisitely crafted ballplaying machine of all time. Manager Joe McCarthy, who loved Gehrig

Lou Gehrig and Joe DiMaggio

The DiMaggio cut

as a son, came to admire DiMaggio with the same paternal pride. He was McCarthy's "perfect player." DiMaggio could do it all. When asked if his perfect player could bunt, the whimsical McCarthy said, "I don't know, nor have I any intention of ever finding out."

Covering the spacious Yankee Stadium center field with grace, speed, and unerring judgment, blessed with a powerful and accurate throwing arm (he led the league in assists his first year; thereafter base runners became wary of him), DiMaggio from the beginning hit with authority and never let up throughout his career. The rookie batted .323, hit 29 home runs, drove in 125 runs, and collected 206 hits, among them 44 doubles and a league-leading 15 triples. He made one of the most emphatic debuts in baseball history. Joe's salary in 1936? Eight thousand dollars.

The veteran Lazzeri gave the club another productive season at second base. Tony's .287 batting average was the lowest among the regulars—an indication of the potency of this lineup. (The team's .483 slugging average was more than 50 points higher than the next club's and almost equaled that of the 1927 team; their 1,065 runs exceeded the 1927 outfit's by 90). Lazzeri batted in 109 runs, the seventh time he had exceeded the 100 mark in runs batted in.

Inspired by the thunder around him, shortstop Frank Crosetti hit for the highest average of his 17-year career—.288. The normally light-hitting Crosetti hit a career-high 15 home runs and also set personal highs for himself in hits, doubles, and runs batted in.

Completing McCarthy's superb infield was third baseman Red Rolfe, a steady, left-handed, line-drive hitter putting in his third full season in pinstripes. Originally a shortstop and converted to third by McCarthy, Red batted .319, led league third basemen in fielding, and tied DiMaggio for the lead with 15 triples. Never a power hitter, the 27-year-old Rolfe took advantage of the deep power alleys of Yankee Stadium, adding 39 doubles to his 15 three-baggers.

Not only did the Yankees have that superb infield, most of whom played at or near the top of their game in 1936, but it remained intact for virtually the entire season. Gehrig, Lazzeri, and Crosetti each appeared in over 150 games, while Rolfe got into 135.

One of the most unenviable jobs in baseball history had fallen to George Selkirk—replacing Babe Ruth in right field for the Yankees. Although a good outfielder who hit with power, George found himself being booed in the beginning through no fault of his own. A legend of Ruth's dimensions simply cannot be replaced; it is gradually molded into memory. To make matters worse, Selkirk was assigned Babe's old No. 3. (Uniform numbers in those days were not retired.)

Nevertheless, Selkirk, nicknamed "Twinkletoes" for his distinctive way of running, accepted the abuse and quietly and determinedly earned his place in the Yankee lineup. In 1936 the 28-year-old left-handed hitter batted .308, hit 18 home runs, and drove in a personal high of 107 runs. Not Ruthian numbers by any means, but surely another solid bat in this potent lineup.

When Joe DiMaggio made his Yankee debut in May 1936 (a spring training injury cost Joe the first 15 games of the season) it was not in center field but left. McCarthy had decided to break in his prize rookie with as little pressure as possible. (Joe had not yet demonstrated his innate immunity to pressure.) Opening the season in center for the club was Ben Chapman, a fiery character whose independent and sometimes abrasive nature had slowly worn down McCarthy's patience. Six weeks into the season the Yankees traded the talented Chapman to the Washington Senators for Jake Powell who was promptly installed in left field with DiMaggio moving over to center.

Jake didn't have any more of a choir boy disposition than Chapman, but McCarthy warmed to Powell's explosive, quick-fisted ways. Joe loved the quiet, gentlemanly Gehrig and profoundly respected the aloof, undemonstrative DiMaggio; but he also had a sneaking fondness

Tony Lazzeri

Red Rolfe

Frank Crosetti

George Selkirk

Jake Powell

Injuries prevented this young man
from going on to a long career
with the Yankees. The club gave
up on him early in 1936 and
traded him to the White Sox. He
later returned to New York for an
outstanding career with the
Brooklyn Dodgers. His name:
Dixie Walker

| Utility outfielder Roy Johnson. This fine veteran got into 63 games and batted .265. | Myril Hoag gave the Yankees some excellent bench strength in 1936. Getting into 45 games Hoag, an outfielder, batted .301. |

for a type like Powell who plunged first into on-the-field brawls. On one occasion, when the club passively accepted some closely thrown pitches by the opposition, McCarthy, wanting to rustle his boys into action, said to Powell, "Jake, are you going to let that pitcher get away with that stuff?" On his next turn at the plate Jake dropped a bunt down the first base line and when the pitcher covered the bag ran right through him, precipitating a good old-fashioned brawl, one of those classic baseball punch-outs in which fifty well-conditioned athletes swing at everyone in sight and inflict little damage.

What McCarthy appreciated above all in Powell, however, was Jake's .306 batting average and perpetual hustle on the bases and in the outfield.

One third of that 1936 Yankee club has appeared on many all-time teams, a remarkable fact in itself. Gehrig is indisputably the game's ranking first baseman, while DiMaggio is the choice of many as the premier center fielder. And the choice of many as baseball's all-time catcher is Bill Dickey.

The tough, soft-spoken, multi-skilled Dickey took over as the Yankees' regular catcher in 1928 and went on to bat over .300 in ten of his first eleven seasons. Like his close friend and roommate Lou Gehrig,

Bill Dickey

Back-up catcher Joe Glenn,
who batted .271 in
1936

Red Ruffing and Joe McCarthy

the Louisiana-born Dickey was durable, setting a record by catching over 100 games for 13 consecutive seasons. He hit for average and he hit with power. In 1936 the man who is arguably the game's greatest catcher had his greatest season, hitting 22 home runs, driving in 107 runs, and setting a major league record for catchers with a .362 batting average.

Generally, the choice as baseball's number one catcher has been between Mickey Cochrane and Dickey. Cochrane's advocates stress, along with his sharp hitting, his running speed and his fiery leadership qualities. Dickey's supporters emphasize his power and the smoothness of his defensive abilities (he led in fielding percentage six times). Bill was also noted for his ability to handle pitchers. When it came to calling a game, Yankee pitcher Spud Chandler recalled, "You didn't argue with Bill Dickey."

The pitching staff that Dickey so ably handled in 1936 was topped by one of the Yankees' fine all-time right-handers, Charley ("Red") Ruffing. In 1936 the 31-year-old Ruffing began the first of four consecutive 20-game seasons with a record of 20–12. His earned run average was 3.85, making him one of the few pitchers in the league to post an

Monte Pearson

Bump Hadley

Lefty Gomez

ERA under four runs per game in that heavy-hitting season. Ruffing, whom the Yankees acquired from the Red Sox in 1930, was also one of the game's better hitting pitchers. Frequently used as a pinch hitter by McCarthy, Charley batted .291 in 1936, including five home runs among his hits. When Ruffing was in the lineup, opposing pitchers had no respite. His bat often kept him in a close game, enabling him to complete 25 of 33 starts.

Although Ruffing was always considered the ace—"He had that stature," one of his teammates said—the most effective pitcher in pinstripes in 1936 was the 26-year-old right-hander Monte Pearson, acquired that year from Cleveland in a trade for pitcher Johnny Allen, a talented but tempestuous character with whom McCarthy finally lost patience. Pearson's 19–7 record gave him the lead in winning percentage, while his 3.71 ERA placed him fifth among American League pitchers.

Remolding their pitching staff with some shrewd trades, the Yankees had in January acquired journeyman right-hander Irving ("Bump") Hadley from the Washington Senators. The 32-year-old Hadley gave the club the best season of his career, chalking up a 14–4 record for a .778 win percentage. Hadley threw hard. A year later, in 1937, an errant Hadley fastball collided with the head of Detroit's player-manager Mickey Cochrane at Yankee Stadium, ending Cochrane's playing career and almost ending his life as well.

McCarthy's 1936 staff was not overwhelmingly strong, though they did lead the league in earned run average and strikeouts, but Joe manipulated them with a sure hand, ending up with six winners in double figures. Lefty Gomez, perhaps the most talented man on the staff, had what for him was a sub-par season with a 13–7 record. Gomez, one of five future Hall of Famers on the team (along with Gehrig, Dickey, Ruffing, and DiMaggio), was noted for both the speed of his fastball and the quickness of his wit. Of the high-ceilinged showers in the rickety clubhouse of old Sportsman's Park in St. Louis, Lefty commented, "By the time the hot water reaches you it's cold." When asked to what he attributed his success, he said, "Clean living and a fast outfield." Toward the end of his career, when it had become apparent the smoke was drifting from his fast one, he was asked if he was still throwing as hard as ever. "Yes," Gomez replied. "But the ball isn't going as fast." When asked by a young pitcher how to play a line drive hit directly back at him, Lefty advised, "Run in on it."

Throughout his career Gomez had the ability—an intangible possessed by many great Yankee pitchers—to win the big games. In Lefty's case this manifested itself most dramatically in his World Series performances where he holds the record for most games won without a loss—six.

Right-hander Johnny Broaca, in his third year with the club,

Pat Malone

Johnny Murphy

Johnny Broaca

logged a 12–7 record. Johnny, the fourth man in the rotation, followed Ruffing, Pearson, and Gomez.

McCarthy's sixth double-figure winner was an old favorite of his from the days when he was managing the Chicago Cubs in the late 1920s, Pat Malone. Pat was one of those hard-drinking, occasionally troublesome types with whom Joe developed a good rapport. One story involving Malone occurred during Prohibition, an era when fellows like Pat sometimes built up man-sized thirsts. It seemed that one night he laid his hands on several bottles of whiskey and took them up to his hotel room with all good intentions. He called down for some ice, but it was delivered in one large block. Impatient, Pat improvised. Putting the block of ice into several pillow cases, he wound up and began smashing it against the wall in order to make chips. By the time the hotel management was pounding on his door, Pat was sitting in his chair sipping whiskey on some pretty jagged rocks.

Malone rejoined his old skipper in New York in 1935 and after a mediocre year gave McCarthy in 1936 his last strong big league season with a 12–4 record, eight of his wins coming in relief. Pat also led the league in saves with nine, a statistic not compiled at the time but retrieved by recent baseball scholarship.

The seventh significant winner on the Yankee pitching staff in 1936 was the man long considered the greatest of all Yankee relief pitchers, Johnny Murphy. The curveballing Murphy, in his third full season in New York, fought off some mid-season injuries and emerged with a 9–3 record and 3.38 earned run average—a glittering figure in that year of the bat in the American League. Between Malone and Murphy the Yankees had by far the strongest bullpen in the league to go along with their solid starting rotation.

This classic combination of heavy hitting, good defense (they tied for second in team fielding), and the fine balance of their mound staff enabled the Yankees in 1936 to dethrone a powerhouse Detroit team gunning for a third straight flag. Although weakened by the loss of their big cannon Hank Greenberg to an early-season injury, the Tigers still fielded a strong-hitting team that featured such stalwarts as Charlie Gehringer, Al Simmons, Gee Walker, and Goose Goslin. Nevertheless, the Yankees steam-rollered the Tigers and the rest of the league, finishing a mammoth 19½ games ahead of second-place Detroit and clinching the pennant on September 9, at the time the earliest winning date in league history. (In 1941 another strong Yankee aggregation lowered the date to September 4.)

The man who made this splendidly proportioned combine run with maximum efficiency himself never played an inning in the big leagues. Philadelphia-born Joseph Vincent McCarthy played in the minor leagues for fifteen years and managed for another seven before taking over the Chicago Cubs in 1926. Let out in Chicago after the 1930 season, he was promptly signed by the Yankees, never ones to let talent linger unemployed for very long.

Joe won his first pennant in New York in 1932, endured three second-place finishes in a row and then pushed into high gear in 1936, winning seven pennants and six World Series in the next eight years. In 1936 his team took the New York Giants in the October pageant in six games. (Joe took the next three Series in 13 games, one over the minimum.)

The McCarthy era saw the molding of the Yankee image of cold, businesslike efficiency. He insisted his players wear ties and jackets on the road and at all times behave like Yankees. He ruled with quiet, unquestioned authority, winning the respect and admiration of his players with his unsurpassed baseball acumen, manipulating his talent with the sureness of a chess grandmaster. His men revered his memory. He never kept charts, never made notes. He kept it all upstairs, they said, and never forgot anything he saw on a ball field.

In an interview given shortly before his death in 1978 at the age of 90, McCarthy was asked what it took to be a manager.

"Just about three things," he replied. "A good memory, patience, and being able to recognize ability. You've got to be able to recognize ability; that's so damned important. And not only recognize it, but to know what to do with it."

Joe McCarthy knew.

The Yankees have just defeated the Giants in the 1936 World Series and become world champions. They would have similar celebrations over the next three years. Front row, left to right: coach Art Fletcher, Joe McCarthy, club owner Jacob Ruppert, rookie Joe DiMaggio

CHAPTER 6

THE 1942
ST. LOUIS CARDINALS

Averaging 26 years of age, they were one of the youngest teams to win a pennant (only the 1914 Boston Braves, with a 24-year age average per man, were younger). They were young and lean and hungry, winning games with an electrifying combination of speed and daring on the bases, a breathtaking defense, and superb pitching. The power hitters batted elsewhere that year—Camilli in Brooklyn, Ott and Mize in New York, Nicholson in Chicago. Enos Slaughter's 13 home runs topped the 1942 St. Louis Cardinals, while rookie Stan Musial hit 10.

One of the most homogeneous of teams, virtually the entire squad were products of the Cardinal farm system, at the time the most far-flung, populous, and fecund in the major leagues. Every regular and all but one of the pitchers had graduated from the top clubs—Columbus of the American Association, Rochester of the International League, or Houston of the Texas League—after having learned their trade at sun-baked way stations like Shelby, North Carolina; New Iberia, Louisiana; Daytona Beach, Florida; Mobile, Alabama; and Greenville, Mississippi.

The Cardinal philosophy, as promulgated by general manager Branch Rickey, was to sign to a contract (usually calling for around $75 a month) any youngster who showed the least glimmer of talent and post him somewhere in a farm system that at one time had as many as 800 players under contract. By the time a player was promoted to the big club, often after five or six years of seasoning, he had undergone the most exacting winnowing process in baseball.

The team was young, but most of the players had gone through a grueling pennant race the year before in which they lost to a tough

Brooklyn Dodger team by 2½ games. Their manager Billy Southworth, 49 years old in 1942 and in his third year at the helm of the Cardinals, had had a 13-year career as a major league outfielder, the last three of them with the Cardinals in the late 1920s. Like his players, Billy had worked his way to the top via the farm system, having successfully managed at Asheville, Columbus, and Rochester. An extremely sound baseball man, he was quiet, friendly, and possessed that absolute necessity required by any manager—the ability to handle men.

One of the hallmarks of a great team is the ability to beat an opponent almost equally good. By this yardstick, the 1942 Cardinals were great and then some. The 1942 Dodgers were a particularly strong club in every respect and were heavy favorites to take a second straight pennant. And for much of that tense, wartime summer they looked unbeatable, winning steadily and impressively. By mid-August they were riding a 10½ game lead over the dogged young Cardinals. Brooklyn general manager Larry MacPhail, however, was far from elated. The normally ebullient and brashly self-confident MacPhail was perturbed by what he perceived as his club's complacency, as well as by the Cardinals' refusal to accept defeat.

It was at about that high-water point in mid-August that MacPhail called his team together in the clubhouse and told them bluntly, "You guys aren't going to win this." Unless they played outstanding ball the rest of the way, he warned, the Cardinals were going to overtake them.

"We could hardly believe what he was saying," Brooklyn second baseman Billy Herman recalled years later. Dodger Dixie Walker offered to bet MacPhail several hundred dollars the team would win by at least eight games. MacPhail refused the bet.

The Dodgers continued to play good, even outstanding, ball. The Cardinals, however, had already begun the most astonishing sustained drive in baseball history, a blistering run that actually consisted of one third of their season as they won 43 of their last 51 games, all of them played under a constantly building pressure. The September records for the two teams were: St. Louis 21–4, Brooklyn 20–5.

"The greatest club I ever played on," said Enos Slaughter of that 1942 Redbird unit. (Slaughter spent 19 seasons in the major leagues, including several with championship Yankee teams in the late 1950s.) "There was tremendous team play and desire; we felt like we just couldn't be beat."

As in 1941, the National League season was highlighted by a series of epic Dodger-Cardinal confrontations, several of them featuring duels between the clubs' aces, Brooklyn's Whitlow Wyatt and the Cardinals' Mort Cooper. The two brilliant right-handers hooked up in St. Louis on the night of August 25 in what remains the classic Dodger-Cardinal game of the early 1940s. Coming into St. Louis with a 7½ game lead, Brooklyn lost the first game of a four-game series to Max Lanier. The following night it was Wyatt versus Cooper. The two grimly determined pitchers matched each other pitch for pitch for twelve scoreless innings. Each club scored a run in the thirteenth, when Wyatt was taken out of the game. In the bottom of the fourteenth the Cardinals scored again, winning 2–1 and cutting Brooklyn's lead to 5½ games, Cooper going the distance.

The following day rookie right-hander Johnny Beazley cut the lead to 4½ with another tension-packed extra inning St. Louis victory, 2–1 in ten. Brooklyn salvaged the final game of the set and left town with a 5½ game lead.

The clubs met next in Brooklyn's Ebbets Field on September 11. The Cardinals arrived with 27 wins in their last 33 games and stood just two games behind. Again Cooper and Wyatt dueled, and again the big St. Louis right-hander won out, blanking the Dodgers 3–0. The following afternoon lefty Max Lanier stopped Brooklyn 2–1 in yet another tensely played game.

The clubs were now deadlocked, the Cardinals having made up a 10½ game deficit in a month. The following day Brooklyn lost a double-header to Cincinnati while the Cardinals were winning in Philadelphia. Southworth's club was in first place, and there they remained, nursing a slim lead down to the finish line, outlasting a fired-up Dodger team that seldom lost a game during a final two-week surge. In winning their pennant the Cardinals won 106 games, the highest National League total since Pittsburgh's 110 in 1909. The second-place Dodgers won 104, the highest win total for a second place finish in league history, and in fact a figure exceeded up to that point only five times in the National League since 1901. But in 1942 it simply was not enough.

The Cardinals' top hitter that year was five-year veteran Enos ("Country") Slaughter, a 26-year-old aggressive, nonstop hustler whose style of play was so admired that future youngsters in his mold were known as "Enos Slaughter types."

The left-handed batting Slaughter, a superb right fielder with a deadly accurate throwing arm, led the club with a .318 average, 13 home runs, 98 runs batted in, 100 runs scored, and had league-leading figures of 188 hits and 17 triples. Slaughter's rise through the Cardinal farm system had been unusually swift, and by the time he reached the big team in 1938 he was still working on a four-year minor league contract he had signed in 1935. The fourth year called for a salary of $400 a month, which was what Slaughter was earning when he reached the big leagues in the spring of 1938, when he learned that the Chicago Cubs had offered the Cardinals $100,000 for him. "They upped me to $600 a month in mid-season," Slaughter recalled. It is doubtful that the payroll for the entire 25-man squad of the 1942 Cardinals exceeded $250,000, about what a utility man is paid today.

In left field St. Louis had a 21-year-old rookie who had come into

Rookie Enos Slaughter (center) at the batting cage at the Cardinals'
spring training camp in 1938. Johnny Mize is on the left, Pepper
Martin on the right. Slaughter was still working on a minor league
contract, earning $400 a month.

their organization in 1938 as a left-handed pitcher. After several years
the promising youngster hurt his arm, but that did not dismay his
employers, for they had already seen him swing a bat. By 1940 he was
a full-time outfielder at Daytona Beach in the Florida State League,
about to make rapid progress. The Cardinals brought him up for the
last few weeks of the 1941 season, unafraid to put him in the lineup in

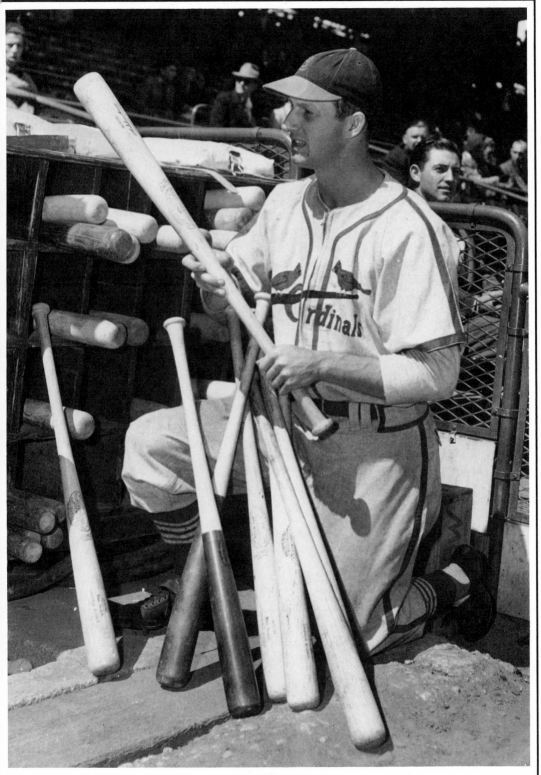

Stan Musial

the waning days of a hard-fought pennant race. Stan Musial responded, splendidly and emphatically, with a .426 batting average for 12 games. One of the greatest careers in National League history had been launched. Some of the Cardinals muttered after the season that Musial should have been brought up sooner, that the slim left-handed hitting youngster and his line drive bat could have made the difference. There was a theory, however, among some of the more cynical Cardinal players, that Branch Rickey, then still running the team, preferred a close second-place finish to winning the pennant, under the reasoning that a long pennant race would stimulate attendance and a second-place finish meant you did not have to hike salaries.

With Musial coming along, the Cardinals had felt confident enough to trade their premier slugger, Johnny Mize, to the New York Giants in the winter of 1941. Low-keyed, likable, unpretentiously self-confident, Musial batted .315 in his first full season, beginning a run of sixteen consecutive seasons of better than .300. (A year later he took the first of his seven batting titles.) Along with his 10 home runs, he had 10 triples and 32 doubles. His .490 slugging average was fourth best in the league.

Center fielder Terry Moore was the third member of the St. Louis outfield. At 30 years of age one of the team's oldest players, Moore had a reputation as the peerless defensive outfielder with an arm so strong his pegs often stung the hands of his infielders. Decades later his teammates would speak with awe and pride of Moore's play in center, with Brooklyn's own brilliant center fielder Pete Reiser saying that Moore's glovework should have earned Terry a niche in the Hall of Fame. A lifetime .280 hitter, Moore batted .288 in 1942.

No outfield ever closed the gaps on a line drive with more élan than the Musial-Moore-Slaughter trio. A rueful Billy Herman recalled that after one of St. Louis' clutch September victories over the Dodgers the uniforms of the Cardinals' outfielders were green from sliding and diving across the Ebbets Field grass in acrobatic theft of Dodger base hits. "I don't know how many extra base hits they took away from us that day," Herman said. "We just couldn't believe what they were doing out there. It got to the point where it just didn't pay to belt one into the outfield."

Nor did it pay to try and ground one through the infield—at least not where shortstop Marty ("Slats") Marion could put his glove on it. At 6'2", the tallest shortstop in the league, Marion ranged from deep in the hole to the first-base side of second picking up would-be base hits with ease and grace. Seldom has a shortstop so dominated an infield. In 1942 the 24-year-old Marion, in his third season, batted .276 and led the league with 38 doubles.

Marion shared the center of the Cardinal infield with two second basemen, Frank ("Creepy") Crespi and Jimmy Brown. Crespi, the only

Terry Moore and Billy Southworth

Enos Slaughter

Marty Marion

Frank (Creepy) Crespi

St. Louis native on the club, was a slick-fielding, light-hitting (.243) second baseman who, like so many of his teammates, got his polish at the Cards' top farm clubs, Columbus and Rochester. Brown, at 32 the club's senior citizen, was a feisty, hustling performer. Jimmy, who batted .256 that year, filled in at three infield positions and did it often enough to end up leading the league with 606 at bats. The switch-hitting Brown had the sharpest eye on the club, striking out only 11 times.

Jimmy Brown   Whitey Kurowski

The regular third baseman was a blond, muscular, 24-year-old rookie, George ("Whitey") Kurowski. Whitey batted .254, and his nine home runs placed him third on the club. One of those home runs beat the Dodgers in a ball game at Ebbets Field in September and locked the Cards and Dodgers into a first-place tie. Whitey hit an even more momentous one in the ninth inning of the fifth and final World Series game against the Yankees that October. The big hit broke a 2–2 tie and gave the Cardinals a 4–2 win and the world championship.

Trading Mize the year before had left a sizable gap at first base, and Southworth filled it by alternating a pair of left-handed-hitting first basemen named Johnny Hopp and Ray Sanders. While neither man hit with Mize's authority, they performed adequately. Hopp, an outfielder the year before, was squeezed out of left field by Musial. He was a speedster who could run with the best of them, and he fit the Cardinal mold perfectly. Johnny, in his third year with St. Louis, batted .258, while the rookie Sanders, the surer glove at first base, hit .252.

Catching the bulk of the games for St. Louis that year was Walker

Ray Sanders

Johnny Hopp

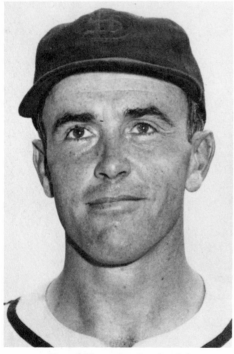

Ken O'Dea, the Cardinals'
second-string catcher
in 1942. He got into 58
games and batted .234.

Cooper, a big, rugged, second-year man who batted .281. One of the outstanding catchers in National League history, Cooper had to spend seven years in the talent-rich Cardinal organization before cracking the top team. Together with his brother Mort, they formed the greatest brother battery in baseball history. A man of awesome strength, Cooper had a playful way of disconcerting opposing hitters when they stepped into the batter's box: he would squirt a stream of tobacco juice across their spikes. "The guy would step out and glare down at Coop," Enos Slaughter said. "Coop would look up at him and say, 'Well, what are you going to do about it?' Here's this giant crouching there, tough as an oak and wearing a mask and chest protector to boot. I'll tell you what they did about it. They did nothing."

Reserve outfielder Harry Walker, who hit .314 that season, got a game whenever he could, unable to break into the Musial-Moore-Slaughter outfield. Harry was a younger brother of Brooklyn's Dixie.

With timely hitting (they led the league in hits, doubles, triples, runs batted in, batting average, and slugging average), spectacular defense, and speed and audacity on the basepaths, the Cardinals were particularly deadly in low-scoring games. And their pitching staff logged a collective earned run average of 2.55 (the lowest in baseball since 1919 and not to be bettered until 1967) that saw to a lot of low-

Harry Walker

Reserve outfielder Coaker Triplett. He got into 64 games in 1942 and batted .273.

The Cardinals' great brother battery. Mort Cooper on the left,
and brother Walker

Johnny Beazley

scoring games. The staff was so deep in talent that a pitcher of the caliber of Harry Brecheen, after five winning seasons in the high minors, still could not crack it.

Mort Cooper, the ace, threw a sharp-breaking fork ball along with a blazing fastball. The 29-year-old Cooper was overpowering that year, winning 22 and losing 7, throwing 10 shutouts (at that time the third highest total in National League history), and posting a scintillating 1.77 league-leading earned run average. Cooper was supreme under pressure, logging a 5–1 record against the hard-hitting Dodgers (overall he was 12–2 versus first division clubs).

Right behind Cooper, a sensational 23-year-old rookie right-hander named Johnny Beazley had finally made the top club after a five-year odyssey through the farm system with stops at Leesburg, Tallahassee, Greenville, Lexington, Abbeville, New Orleans, Montgomery, Columbus, and Mobile. After this tour of America's ball yards young Beazley was determined to stick and came through with a brilliant 21–6 season and a 2.13 earned run average. Beazley's career was then interrupted by military service. He injured his arm during the war and never pitched the same again.

Left-hander Max Lanier was 13–8 with a 2.96 earned run average, and most important was 5–2 against the Dodgers. Relief pitchers

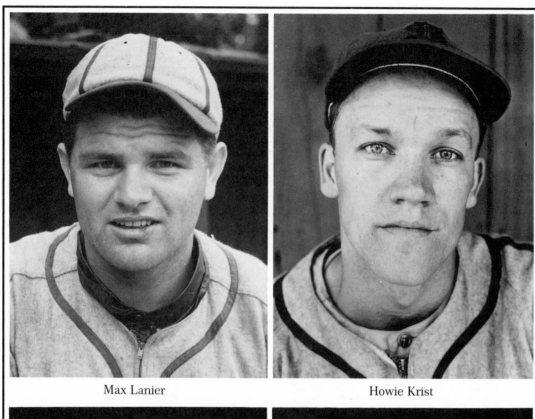

Max Lanier

Howie Krist

Harry Gumbert

Howie Pollett

Ernie White   Murry Dickson

Howie Krist and Harry Gumbert (the only regular performer who had not been graduated from a farm club) were effective with 13–3 and 9–5 records respectively. A stylish 21-year-old lefty named Howie Pollett rounded out the staff with 7–5 and a 2.89 ERA, along with another left-hander, Ernie White, who was also 7–5, with a 2.53 ERA. White, a club ace the year before, suffered from a sore arm much of the year. Also operating out of the bullpen most of the year was a trim right-hander named Murry Dickson who was 6–3 with a 2.90 ERA. Topped by Cooper's 10, the Cardinal staff led the league with 18 shutouts.

Trained together on the minor league grounds of the Cardinal farm system, this club played, as one observer put it, "like one man." Woefully underpaid, they kept their eyes steadfastly focused on that World Series money because, as Mort Cooper said, "We flat out needed it." And they knew too, that right behind them, laboring at Rochester and Columbus and Houston, were other equally hungry and almost as equally talented youngsters determined to break into the lineup.

They kept hustling that October, right into the bared teeth of a powerful Yankee team. Joe McCarthy's club had taken its sixth pen-

The heart of Billy Southworth's great pitching staff in 1942.
From left to right, Max Lanier, Ernie White, Mort Cooper,
Johnny Beazley, Harry Gumbert

nant in seven years and was undefeated in World Series play covering eight appearances since 1926.

The Yankees were led by Joe DiMaggio, the greatest of modern ballplayers. Behind the Yankee Clipper the squad included Joe Gordon, Phil Rizzuto, Charlie Keller, and Bill Dickey. The Yankee pitching staff was headed by 21-game winner Ernie Bonham, Spud Chandler, Hank Borowy, and Red Ruffing. The New Yorkers were overwhelming favorites.

Ruffing beat the Cardinals in the opener, 7–4, pitching no-hit ball into the eighth inning. The four St. Louis runs came in a ninth inning rally that left the Cardinals not depressed but instead bursting with confidence. They had thrown a scare into the lordly Yankees.

The following day Beazley evened the Series with a 4–3 win. Moving to New York, Ernie White pitched the game of his life with a left arm so numb "You could have stuck a fork in it and I wouldn't have felt it," shutting out the Yankees 2–0. In the seventh inning White needed, and received, some help from his outfield. On successive at-bats, Musial took a home run away from Gordon with a leaping catch in front of the left field stands, and then Slaughter robbed Keller of a home run with an even more spectacular leap in front of the right field stands.

Unstoppable now, the Cardinals out-slugged the Yankees 9–6 the next day, with three innings of airtight relief pitching by Lanier sealing the victory. The next day Beazley ended it with his second complete game win, 4–2, the winning runs coming in on Kurowski's two-run shot in the ninth.

This marvelous ball-playing unit went on to take three more pennants and two world championships in the next four years until finally dethroned by the burgeoning Brooklyn dynasty that began forming in the late 1940s.

Recalling the 1942 St. Louis Cardinals, one finds memories of a team that simply would not be beaten, a team that seldom pulverized anyone but that habitually scored just enough runs to win. Few clubs have ever attacked with such sure baseball sense or such splendidly spirited self-confidence.

CHAPTER 7

THE 1953 BROOKLYN DODGERS

Between 1947 and 1956 the Brooklyn Dodgers won six pennants, had three second-place finishes and one third. Playing most of those years with a set lineup that was at times virtually an all-star team, the Dodgers were the National League's dominant force for a decade.

Few teams in all of baseball history ever possessed as much championship balance and versatility as these Brooklyn clubs; and among those teams the 1953 squad was especially strong. This remarkable unit of smooth and gifted professionals led the National League in runs and runs batted in for the fifth consecutive time, home runs for the fifth consecutive time, slugging average for the fifth consecutive time, stolen bases for the eighth consecutive time, fielding average for the third consecutive time, and their pitchers led the league in strike-outs for the sixth consecutive time. (An interesting footnote: Dodger pitchers, in Brooklyn and Los Angeles, led all National League staffs in strikeouts for sixteen consecutive years, 1948 through 1963.)

Brooklyn totally dominated the National League in 1953. Winning 105 games and losing 49, they finished 13 games ahead of a solid Milwaukee Braves team that featured stars like Eddie Mathews, Joe Adcock, Del Crandall, Andy Pafko, and Johnny Logan, and pitchers Warren Spahn, Lew Burdette, Bob Buhl, and Johnny Antonelli. The Dodgers' .285 team batting average was 12 points higher than the next club's; their stolen base total was almost double that of the next highest figure; their .474 slugging average was 50 points above the next club's and one of the highest in major league history; their 208 home runs constituted the second highest total ever in the major leagues.

The team had been carefully built by Brooklyn's (and baseball's) resident genius, Branch Rickey. Because of the dimensions of Ebbets Field, Rickey stocked the club with right-hand power like Gil Hodges, Roy Campanella, Jackie Robinson, and Carl Furillo. The club's merciless consumption of left-handed pitching brought them an almost steady diet of right-handers, helping their one lefty-swinging power man Duke Snider to become one of the league's most devastating hitters.

The Dodgers were still reaping the rewards of Rickey's courageous and farsighted introduction of black players into the major leagues in 1947. By 1953 Rickey's revolution was still of limited impact, with only the Giants and Braves among National League teams showing a black player regularly in their starting lineup. In 1953 one third of Brooklyn's starting nine were black, the club having broken gifted rookie Jim Gilliam into the lineup along with established regulars Robinson and Campanella, while relief pitcher Joe Black was the only nonwhite hurler to appear in a National League game that year.

Under Manager Chuck Dressen, a chipper character whose egomania charmed rather than offended his team of hard-nosed professionals, the Dodgers played solid ball all season, pursued by the Braves through much of the summer. At the end of June the Braves stood a half game behind the first place Dodgers, but then in July and August

Manager Chuck Dressen

Jackie Robinson

Bobby Morgan, on the left, would have been the regular third baseman on many clubs. But on this club the third basemen were Jackie Robinson, shown here talking to Morgan, and Billy Cox.

the Brooklyn club began to soar, running up a 48–14 record through those two months, finally losing the Braves in mid-August and coasting home in September to their 13-game victory margin.

After leaving the St. Louis Cardinals to take over the Dodgers in 1943, Rickey began building for Brooklyn the same kind of far-flung minor league organization from which he had stocked Cardinal teams for nearly two decades. Soon after the war was over the farm clubs at Montreal, St. Paul, Fort Worth, and all the way down the line to places like Olean, New York, and Valdosta, Georgia, began producing Brooklyn-bound ballplayers in quantity. Almost the entire roster in 1953—almost all of the players of that incomparable decade of Brooklyn baseball—were harvested from the farm system.

Jackie Robinson, 34 years old in 1953, was still one of the team's driving forces and its most vivid personality. After several years of suppressing his simmering emotions and fierce combative manner in deference to Rickey's "experiment," Jackie had become a blunt, outspoken foe of discrimination, bigotry, and just about anything else that upset him. No longer did opposing pitchers throw at him with impunity nor base runners come at him with raised spikes. Knowing that many still resented and disliked him for having been the first black in the major leagues, Robinson frequently went out of his way to taunt the opposition with false starts on the basepaths that he frequently followed with daring bursts of speed as he moved from base to base. He performed relentlessly, a dynamic factor in every game he played, whether at bat, on the bases, or in the field.

After years as the team's regular second baseman, Robinson had agreed to move over to open that spot for the rookie Gilliam. As a result, the versatile Jackie played half the season in left field and the remainder of his games at third base, with a few appearances at second and first. He had one of his best years in 1953, batting .329 and driving in 95 runs, one of five Dodgers to drive in over 90 runs that year. In scoring 109 times, Jackie was one of six Dodgers to score 100 runs, a major league team record. In the matter of run production, only three clubs in National League history have ever topped Brooklyn's 955 runs scored in 1953, and all three did it in the haywire year of 1930 when the league as a whole batted .303. In 1953 the National League batted .266.

At first base the Dodgers had one of the National League's all-time greats at the position, Gil Hodges. Another product of the farm system, the versatile Hodges came up as a third baseman, switched to catching, and in 1948 took over first base, a position he played flawlessly—he was considered, in fact, the paragon of defensive first basemen. A man of imposing physical strength (as a manager years later his brooding silences could intimidate his players), Hodges was one of the heavy generators in the Brooklyn power system. Driving in over 100 runs for

Gil Hodges

Twenty-two-year-old Wayne
Belardi was a power-hitting
first baseman, but so
was Gil Hodges. Playing
when he could, the
youngster batted .239
with 11 homes runs.

Roy Campanella

Reserve catcher Rube Walker.
He was strong on defense and
could hit with power, but the man
in front of him was named
Roy Campanella.

seven consecutive seasons (1949–1955), he put together one of his better years in 1953, hitting 31 home runs, driving in 122 runs, and batting .302—one of five .300 hitters in Dressen's lineup.

More heavy thunder came from behind the plate where Roy Campanella crouched in the very heart of a Hall of Fame career. Surely among the half dozen greatest catchers in baseball history, Roy won his second Most Valuable Player Award in 1953 (he won a third in 1955). A superb defensive rock behind the plate, Campanella possessed an arm mighty in strength and accuracy. Brooklyn pitchers in those years testified to the fact that Campy's sureness behind the plate helped build their self-confidence. After years of learning his trade in the Negro leagues, he entered the Brooklyn organization at the same time as Robinson, with Nashua of the New England League. He joined the big team in mid-season 1948 after integrating the American Association with the St. Paul club. It was Campanella's arrival that moved the talent-rich Dodgers to transfer Hodges to first base.

Campanella's bat smote with record-breaking fury that year. His 41 home runs and 142 runs batted in remain all-time peaks for major league catchers. Catching 140 games, the durable Campanella batted .312 and led National League catchers with a .989 fielding percentage.

Still another farm club product on this team of high achievers was center fielder Edwin ("Duke") Snider. The 26-year-old Snider was in the prime of a career that would culminate with his election to the Hall of Fame. Like so many of his teammates, Snider was the complete ballplayer, combining a potent bat with outstanding running speed and impeccable defensive work. Confined by the neighborly walls of Ebbets Field, this exquisite outfielder showed the full range of his ball-hawking abilities when he played in the broad expanses of parks like the Polo Grounds and Yankee Stadium, running down the long ones with the ease and grace of a DiMaggio.

Snider, who once excited the sensibilities of baseball fans by confessing he played the game for the money (today a man would rate headlines by asserting otherwise), poled 42 home runs in 1953, giving the Dodgers the distinction of becoming the first team in National League history to have two men hit 40 or more home runs in a single season. A power hitter who also hit for average, Snider batted .336, drove in 126 runs, scored a league-leading 132 times, and posted a .627 slugging average, also a league-leading figure.

In addition to winning the pennant and leading the league in home runs, hits, runs, stolen bases, batting average, slugging average, and having the individual leaders in runs batted in (Campanella), runs scored (Snider), slugging (Snider), and triples (Gilliam), the 1953 Dodgers also had the league batting champion, right fielder Carl Furillo, who hit .344.

The rugged Furillo was one of the few Dodgers whose professional

Duke Snider

George Shuba, reserve outfielder
and pinch hitter deluxe

Don Thompson, a reserve
outfielder on the '53
Dodgers. He was light
of stick (.242) but
brilliant on defense.

Carl Furillo

Spectators at the Furillo-Durocher brawl. Carl and Leo are out of
sight on the grass. Despite the appearance of belligerence, all of
the gentlemen above were peacemakers—a rare instance of peacemakers
outnumbering combatants—and no other blows were struck in anger.

experience predated Rickey's arrival, having signed with the Brooklyn
organization as an 18-year-old in 1940. Furillo emerged from the service in 1945, made the team in spring training 1946, and quickly established himself as a brilliant outfielder with one of the strongest
throwing arms ever seen in the big leagues—several times in his career
he achieved the rare feat of throwing out a batter on what appeared to
be a base hit to right field.

Furillo was serious-minded, a good man, but not one to tamper
with. After having been hit several times by pitched balls he became,
understandably, resentful at being thrown at. This leads to the story of
his batting title. Furillo, who only once in 14 seasons batted under .284,
played in 132 games in 1953. In game 132, against the Giants at the
Polo Grounds, Carl stood at the plate, Giants pitcher Ruben Gomez
stood on the mound, and Giants manager Leo Durocher stood in the
dugout. Carl and Leo were not the best of friends. Leo ordered Gomez
to "stick it in his ear." The "it" was the baseball, and the ear belonged

to Furillo. Furillo heard the command and a moment later felt the baseball, not in his ear but in his ribs.

Furillo did not journey to first base placidly. On the way he shared with Leo his thoughts on Leo's fortitude and ancestry. Never one to shrink from debate, Leo answered in kind. There were warnings, threats, and finally an invitation to engage in mayhem. Carl charged off of first base and met Leo in combat in front of the Giants' dugout. When the dust had settled, Furillo left the game with a broken hand and a batting average frozen for the remainder of the season at .344. The Cardinals' Stan Musial and Red Schoendienst took aim at this ripe, stationary target that September, but each came up short, Red by two points, Stanley by five. Along with his unconquerable batting mark, Furillo weighed in with 21 home runs and 92 runs batted in, standard numbers for this prince among ballplayers who was constantly being overshadowed by some of his more majestic teammates.

The Dodgers' 24-year-old switch-hitting rookie second baseman Jim Gilliam had achieved the near-impossible—forcing his way onto this team of all-stars (both the '52 and '53 Dodger clubs placed six regulars on the National League All-Star teams). After two years at Montreal the talented and versatile Gilliam, who gave the Dodgers ser-

Jim Gilliam   Billy Cox

vice at second, third, and the outfield during his career, joined the club and was voted Rookie of the Year on the strength of his .278 batting average and league-leading 17 triples. The sharp-eyed rookie also drew 100 bases on balls, second highest total in the league.

At third base this team of superlative defensive ballplayers had one of the most gifted glovemen in the game's history, position notwithstanding. His name was Billy Cox. He was 33 years old, frail, sickly (he had never fully recovered from the malaria he contracted during the war), and in 1953 near the end of his career. Nevertheless he got into 100 games and batted .291, his highest mark ever.

Cox was obtained, along with left-hander Preacher Roe, from the Pittsburgh Pirates after the 1947 season in one of Branch Rickey's most notable deals. In return for Cox and Roe, Rickey sent Pittsburgh 37-year-old outfielder Dixie Walker and pitchers Hal Gregg and Vic Lombardi, none of whom contributed much to the Pirates.

Billy could backhand scorchers down the line with a quickness and agility sportswriters repeatedly called "catlike," go to his left with a crisp grace, and fire the ball to first with an arm whose strength belied his slightness of frame. Brooks Robinson was the greatest defensive third baseman the game has ever seen—except, say many, for Brooklyn's Billy Cox.

The heart of the 1953 Brooklyn team—and of many other Brooklyn teams—was the club's captain and shortstop, Harold ("Pee Wee") Reese. The team's veteran—he was obtained from the Boston Red Sox' Louisville farm club in 1940—Reese was every inch the poised, seasoned professional. His managers measured him by his intangibles as much as by his solid and consistent on-the-field performances. His teammates looked to him for guidance and leadership. When some outspoken hostility to Jackie Robinson's joining the club erupted in 1947, the Kentuckian Reese's graceful acceptance of Jackie made life just a little easier for the new man, something Robinson appreciated and never forgot.

Reese was a winning ballplayer in every sense of the word. He made the big plays in the field, he was dangerous in the clutch, hit with adequate power, moved runners along when he needed to, and was an extremely shrewd baserunner, consistently among the leaders in stolen bases. In 1953, then 34 years old, he batted .271 and was second in stolen bases with 22 (Gilliam was third, Robinson fourth, and Snider fifth, behind Milwaukee's Bill Bruton who led the league with 26 in this era when the art of stealing bases was temporarily at a low ebb). Pee Wee hit 13 home runs, one of eight Dodgers in double figures in home runs that year.

Charlie Dressen's pitching staff was topped by 26-year-old Carl Erskine who had his finest year in 1953. The trimly built right-hander had a 20–6 record and the league's best winning percentage, .769.

Pee Wee Reese

Carl Erskine

Handsome, intelligent, articulate, Erskine was a dogged competitor on the mound. Mixing a good fastball with a sharp overhand curve, a virtuoso at changing speeds, he pitched brilliantly. His 187 strikeouts placed him second to Philadelphia's Robin Roberts.

Colorful right-hander Russ Meyer, acquired from the Phillies that year, gave the Dodgers a strong 15–5 season. A volatile character who featured a screwball in his repertoire, Meyer once threw a rosin bag into the air to express his displeasure at an umpire's call. The bag came down and hit Russ on the head. "Sure he was a little strange," Dressen said of the man they called "The Mad Monk." "But he always wanted the ball. He always wanted to pitch." Charlie's kind of pitcher.

Billy Loes, another righty who, according to Campanella, had the best assortment of breaking pitches on the staff, was another singular character. The 23-year-old Loes, a New York City product and graduate of the farm system, was moody, maybe a bit eccentric (he predicted the Yankees in six in that year's World Series; to his dismay he was right), but he could be awfully tough on the mound. In 1953 he was 14–8. Most important, Billy was 5–1 against the team's chief rival that year, Milwaukee.

The 38-year-old Preacher Roe, acquired from Pittsburgh along with Cox, had his last productive season with this great team, the first Dodger team in history to win two consecutive pennants. Roe's career record with Brooklyn was a remarkable 93–37; in 1953 the canny lefty was 11–3. Roe, whose square name was Elwin, shocked some people years after his retirement by admitting he had on occasion thrown a spitter. At that time many fans retained a naive attitude that this was "cheating," an attitude that evaporated with the advent of high salaries, renegotiated contracts, and designated hitters, relegating Preacher's confession to the catalogue of venial sins.

Eighteen years younger than Roe, another left-hander, a 20-year-old rookie named Johnny Podres, two years later would bring the ultimate glory to Brooklyn baseball by shutting out the Yankees in the seventh game of the World Series, giving the club its one and only world title. In 1953 the fastballing youngster, shrewdly brought along by Dressen, was 9–4. Johnny was another farm club product. (Of the team's front-liners that year only Reese, Meyer, Roe, and Cox were not developed by the Dodger organization.)

The Brooklyn bullpen was exceptionally strong in 1953. The number one man was righty Clem Labine, probably the greatest relief pitcher Brooklyn ever had. He threw a devastating sinker, putting to work those superb gloves in the infield behind him. When Clem was in the game few balls were lifted into the air, a singular virtue when one took into account the cozy dimensions of the Ebbets Field walls. Labine was 11–6, with a 2.78 earned run average, the best on the staff.

Along with Labine in the bullpen were fastballers Jim Hughes, 4–

Russ Meyer

Billy Loes

Preacher Roe

Johnny Podres

Clem Labine

Jim Hughes

Bob Milliken

3 with nine saves; Bob Milliken, 8–4; Ben Wade, 7–5; and Joe Black who had had a brilliant rookie year in 1952 but who pitched with only intermittent success in 1953.

Dressen's strength as a manager lay in handling pitchers, and he never did it better than in 1953. With his ace Don Newcombe in his second and final year of military service, Charlie manipulated and spotted his pitchers with year-long success.

It was the bats, gloves, and running speed of this team, however, that earned it its place among the most memorable in baseball history. The collective talents of the 1953 Brooklyn Dodgers have seldom been equaled. In his decades in baseball Branch Rickey put together many outstanding teams, but none to compare to his 1953 pennant winners in Brooklyn.

CHAPTER 8

THE 1961
NEW YORK YANKEES

In 1961 American League fans awaited the opening of the baseball season with special interest and anticipation. After undergoing several franchise shifts during the past half dozen years, the league had now taken the even more radical step of expanding from eight teams to ten. The Washington Senators had become the Minnesota Twins, with a brand new team moving into the nation's capital; and the American League had finally followed the National to the West Coast, placing a team in Los Angeles. In addition, the venerable 154-game schedule had been stretched to 162 games.

Yankee fans had additional curiosity because of a new manager. After winning 10 pennants in 12 years, the 70-year-old Casey Stengel had been let go by employers who considered him too old. ("I'll never make the mistake of being seventy again," quipped Mr. Stengel.) His replacement, 41-year-old, long-time organization man Ralph Houk, had served the team as player, minor league manager, and coach. Houk, called "The Major" for his wartime service in the Rangers, was a sound baseball man and a rugged character whom the players admired and respected. Unlike Stengel, Houk never criticized his men in public nor did he go out of his way to pander to the press and seek the limelight, traits of Stengel's that had grown increasingly irritating to those around him.

Having inherited a team that played power baseball, Houk let his players swing away. The 1961 Yankees stole just 28 bases, and 21 of those were stolen by two men, Mickey Mantle (12) and Bobby Richardson (9). Three regulars stole no bases—Bill Skowron, Elston Howard, and Roger Maris. Two regulars, Tony Kubek and Clete Boyer, stole one base apiece, while Yogi Berra stole two.

In truth, Houk's boys didn't need to run very much that year. Why run when you could trot? And trot they did, as they became the focus of the American League with the most thunderous season-long home-run cannonade in major league history. By season's end records were falling every time another Yankee home run left the ball park. A new all-time single season home-run record was established with 240 long shots, breaking by a healthy 47 the league record set just the year before by Stengel's team in a 154-game schedule. In establishing their new standard, the Yankees hit 112 homers at home and 128 on the road.

Six men on that team hit 20 or more home runs, two men hit over 50 home runs, 10 pinch hitters hit home runs, 24 times a single player hit two home runs in a game. All records. Overshadowing it all, however, was the unprecedented slugging show put on by outfielders Mickey Mantle and Roger Maris. Batting back-to-back in the lineup, Maris third and Mantle fourth, they accounted for a two-man record 115 home runs, 61 for Roger, 54 for Mickey.

Twenty-six-year-old Roger Maris had been obtained after the 1959

Ralph Houk in the
late 1940s

season in a trade with the Kansas City Athletics, at the time a scandalous trading partner with the Yankees. Between 1953 and 1960 the Yankees and Athletics engaged in 17 separate deals involving 68 players. The relationship between the clubs has never been satisfactorily explained, but Kansas City, once a minor league farm club of the Yankees, had become virtually a major league farm club of the Yankees. No less than nine men on the New York team in 1961 had been acquired from Kansas City (some of them reacquisitions).

The Maris trade was the culmination of the New York-Kansas City wheeling and dealing. A left-handed pull hitter with a stroke tailor-made for Yankee Stadium's inviting right field seats, Roger had had an excellent season in 1960 with 39 home runs, a league-leading 112 runs batted in, and the Most Valuable Player Award. Good as that was, it in no way prepared anyone for the astounding performance he put on in 1961. Not since Joe DiMaggio's hitting streak in 1941 did a player hold the baseball nation in thrall for so extended a period.

After going homerless through his first ten games, Roger began finding the range. At the end of May he had 12 homers, at the end of June (during which he hit 15 home runs, a league record for that month), he had 27. At the end of July he had 40 seat-busters, six ahead of Ruth's record pace when the Babe hit 60 in 1927. At the end of August he had 51, eight ahead of Ruth for the same period. At the end

Roger Maris

Maris hitting No. 61

of the club's 155th game, he had 59—this would have marked the end of what had previously been the normal season's schedule (the team had played one tie). The games' traditionalists breathed a sigh of relief —Ruth's record was still intact.

He had eight more games to play, however, and Roger fueled the fires of controversy by hitting number 60 in game 159 and number 61 in game 163, the season's last. The achievement has caused a double entry in the record books—Ruth's 60 for the 154-game season, Maris's 61 for the extended season.

Maris, whose heavy hitting overshadowed his excellence as a right fielder, added to his season's luster with a league-leading 142 runs batted in and another Most Valuable Player trophy.

In spite of his history-making season, Maris never won the popularity he deserved in New York. His monumental season never got him

Mickey Mantle

Power plus: Mickey Mantle

| Bill Skowron | Yogi Berra |

the acclaim or adulation accorded Ruth, Gehrig, DiMaggio, or his team-mate Mantle.

Mickey, as his predecessor in center field DiMaggio had been, was the heart of the Yankees, the number one slugger, the image, the inspirational player. Fan adulation for Mickey was so intense by 1961 that they seemed to have none left over for anyone else.

Mickey Mantle is one of the titans of Yankee legend. Like Ruth, Gehrig, and DiMaggio before him, he grew to larger-than-life propor-tions in Yankee pinstripes. Mantle was perhaps the most abundantly gifted of all ballplayers: he hit with stunning power from either side of the plate, had a strong throwing arm, and possessed running speed remarkable for any athlete, much less a home run hitter. This unprec-edented combination of power and speed, plus a stoicism in the face of the pain of the many injuries he sustained in his long career, captivated the imaginations of baseball fans everywhere, and most compellingly in New York. He was with Willie Mays the game's most exciting and explosive performer for more than a decade, and one of its premier drawing cards.

The Oklahoma-born Mantle, signed to a Yankee farm club contract in 1949 for a bonus of around $1,100, had one of his most spectacular seasons in 1961. Swinging behind Maris all season—a decided advantage for Roger who had to be pitched to in spite of his scorching home run bat—Mantle kept pace with him through most of the summer until slowed by a September injury. Mickey hit 54 home runs, the sixth highest single season total in big league history, and drove in 128 runs. He batted .317 and led the league with a .687 slugging average. He also drew the most walks, 126. He was the most feared hitter since Ted Williams, averaging one walk per five at bats. Maris drew one walk per seven at bats.

The third most productive long-ball hitter on this most prolific of home-run-hitting teams was first baseman Bill Skowron. Playing in his eighth year in New York, the right-handed-hitting Skowron saw much of his power neutralized by the vast left and center fields in Yankee Stadium. He compensated, however, by demonstrating unusual power to right-center where many of his home run shots went in the stadium. The muscular Skowron hit 28 full-distance blasts while batting .267 and driving in 89 runs.

Fourth place in the Yankee home run circus in that record-shattering season was held by 36-year-old Lawrence Peter Berra whose unforgettable nickname "Yogi" has transcended baseball and made him known to all Americans, baseball fans or not. Then playing the outfield most of the time, after more than a decade behind the plate, the veteran

Elston Howard

Hector Lopez, just before being traded to the Yankees. A solid hitter, Lopez was unable to break into the starting lineup in 1961.

Berra, after Ruth probably the most beloved of all Yankee players, still swung a potent bat. Yogi hit 22 home runs and batted .271.

Berra was considered the team's most dangerous clutch hitter, Mantle notwithstanding. Yogi's .270 average could be misleading. Informed one year by a New York newspaperman that Yogi was swinging below par, Baltimore Orioles manager Paul Richards suggested the man check the records and see what Berra was hitting from the seventh inning on. The next day the man sheepishly reported to Richards that from the seventh inning on Berra was batting over .430.

Along with malapropisms and an ingenuous charm, the Berra myth included a legendary facility for hitting bad balls. The veteran pitcher Warren Spahn disputed this. Spahn, who had pitched to him many times, claimed Yogi was a guess hitter and that when he guessed right he was going to swing no matter where the ball was pitched. However, Spahn said, in a tight spot when Berra was really bearing down at the plate you had to throw him strikes because Yogi actually had perfect bat control and full command of the strike zone.

The Yankees' leading batter in 1961 was catcher Elston Howard. Howard, who in 1955 had become the team's first black player, had his finest season in 1961, batting .348 and hitting 21 home runs. The 32-year-old right-handed-hitting Howard, a product of the Yankee farm system, was a remarkably versatile player. An outfielder when he joined the team in 1955, he filled in at first base while gradually taking over the regular catching duties from the aging Berra.

Batting behind Maris and Mantle who, as Ruth and Gehrig had done in 1927, frequently left the bases swept clean, Howard still managed to drive in 77 runs. He was a sharp hitter and a dangerous one, and his .348 batting average that year certainly left pitchers no respite after the ordeal of having faced Maris and Mantle.

By 1961 Bobby Richardson had established himself as one of the fine second basemen in Yankee history. Brought along through the farm system, the compact, smooth-fielding Richardson was a sharp-eyed contact hitter at the top of the lineup. If he walked infrequently, at least he seldom struck out (only 23 times in 662 at bats in 1961), batting .261 in the big home run year but between his walks and base hits reaching base over 200 times, giving him inestimable value in that power-laden lineup. Consistently steady in the field, Bobby led American League second basemen four times in double plays, including 1961.

At shortstop in 1961 the Yankees had a man considered by some knowledgeable baseball men as the finest in club annals, Phil Rizzuto notwithstanding. By 1961 the 24-year-old Tony Kubek was already in his fifth big league season. Until he was forced into premature retirement in 1965 because of an injury, Kubek was one of the most versatile men on the club, a fact cherished and exploited by the manipulative

Tony Kubek

Bobby Richardson

Clete Boyer

126

Clete Boyer made this spectacular play in the second game of
the 1961 World Series against Cincinnati. He recovered in
time to throw the batter out.

Stengel who moved Tony back and forth between the infield and out-field. When Houk took over, however, he nailed Kubek into the short-stop position and kept him there.

Kubek covered large swatches of ground—he led American League shortstops in total chances in 1961—and possessed a strong throwing arm. Swinging a solid if unobtrusive bat in the Yankees' dy-namite lineup, he batted .276, collected 170 hits, and tied for second place in the league with 38 doubles, an unusually high amount for a shortstop.

Third baseman Clete Boyer completed one of the premier defensive infields ever for the Yankees. Boyer, who was obtained from the Kansas City Athletics in 1959 (after the A's had paid him a handsome bonus to sign), was outstanding in every respect at third base. Quick-handed with flawless instincts, his arm was strong and accurate. With a .224 batting average, the 24-year-old Boyer was the lone oasis for opposing pitchers in the Yankee batting order that year, though he did generate enough power to add 11 home runs to the team's record total.

The club's sixth 20-homer man was not even a regular; in fact he had less than a half season's worth of at-bats. Johnny Blanchard was a catcher, outfielder, and pinch hitter with a wicked left-handed swing designed for the stadium's inviting right-field porch. Coming to bat just 243 times, Blanchard hit 21 homers and drove in 54 runs, with a bat-ting average of .305.

Actually, Houk's team differed little from Stengel's 1960 pennant winners. The significant difference lay in the pitching staff, and how the manager employed it. The ace that year was the greatest of all Yankee pitchers, the New York-born left-hander Edward Charles ("Whitey") Ford. Signed for a small bonus and sent through the farm system, Ford came up in 1950, won his first nine straight, and started on his way to Cooperstown.

A master craftsman on the mound, Whitey threw an assortment of sharply-darting breaking pitches that were almost impossible to lift into the air. In 1961 this all-time Yankee pitcher reached the very summit of his career. Before Houk's arrival, Stengel generally had spotted his almost unbeatable ace against certain pitchers and certain teams, often holding Whitey out of turn. Under Houk's stewardship, Ford took his turn with unbroken regularity. As a consequence, Whitey started far more games than he had under Stengel and won far more games. Under Stengel his top win total had been 19; in 1961 the 32-year-old Ford put together a spectacular 25–4 record for a league-leading .862 win percentage.

Behind Ford in the win column was 25-year-old right-hander Ralph Terry. Terry had been developed in the Yankee farm system, traded to Kansas City where he served his big league apprenticeship, and then reacquired in 1959. In 1961 Terry racked up a nearly flawless

Johnny Blanchard

Ralph Terry

Whitey Ford, so superior to other pitchers that they called
him "The Chairman of the Board"

Luis Arroyo

Bob Turley. The one-time Yankee
ace suffered arm problems in
1961 and slumped to a 3–5 record.

Hal Reniff. He was second man
out of the bullpen behind
Arroyo in 1961.

130

16–3 record for an .842 winning percentage, giving the team two pitchers who combined for a 41–7 won-lost record.

The club's third big winner that year was one of those pleasant surprises that occasionally occur, Luis Arroyo. After a nondescript career in the National League, Arroyo was picked up after the 1959 season from Cincinnati. He pitched well in relief in 1960, but in 1961 the left-handed, screwball-throwing Arroyo was a magician coming out of the bullpen. The portly 34-year-old veteran appeared in 65 games, all in relief, won 15, lost 5, and saved 29 others. (Arroyo's glory did not last beyond 1961; a year later he was 1–3 and the year after that he was gone.)

Houk's other winners were three righties out of the farm system: Bill Stafford, 14–9; Jim Coates, 11–5; and rookie Rollie Sheldon, 11–5.

In addition to leading the league with their record-shattering home run total and having the league's top starting and relief pitchers, this finely balanced Yankee club also led in least errors, most double plays, and highest fielding percentage. It was a stunning coming together of dynamic talents—Mantle, Maris, Howard, Ford—each enjoying their most productive seasons in the big leagues.

In spite of this powerful surge, and in spite of winning 109 games —the third highest total in American league history—Houk's club was locked in a season-long struggle with a strong Detroit club. On September 1 the Tigers, just a game and a half back, came to New York to play a showdown three-game series.

The three games, which drew over 170,000 fans, broke the hearts and spirits of the Tigers. Ford and Arroyo combined to win the opener 1–0 on a ninth inning single by Skowron. The next day Maris's 52nd and 53rd home runs and a strong relief effort by Arroyo stopped Detroit 7–2. The day after that the Yankees broke the backs of the Tigers once and for all, winning 8–5. Losing 5–4 in the last of the ninth, the New Yorkers tied it on Mantle's fiftieth round-tripper and won it a few moments later on a three-run shot by Elston Howard. The Tigers went on to win 101 games but still finished eight games behind Houk's fence-busters.

This mightiest of all home run teams continued its hard hitting in the World Series against Cincinnati, taking the Reds easily in five games, hitting seven home runs along the way.

The 1961 New York Yankees had taken the team's tradition—the tradition of Ruth and Gehrig and DiMaggio—and lifted it to heights never scaled before, and never equaled since.

CHAPTER 9

THE 1969
BALTIMORE ORIOLES

Few teams have had the combination of power, pitching, and defense that the Baltimore Orioles had in 1969. This was Manager Earl Weaver's greatest team, winner of 109 games, a team that finished 19 games ahead of second-place Detroit in the American League's East Division in that first year of divisional play.

Weaver had four solid starting pitchers and a well-stocked bullpen; at the plate he had a team that hit for power (four men with over 20 home runs), for average (six men over .280), and that struck out fewer times than any team in the league. In the field his superlative defense was highlighted by three of the most dazzling glovemen in the game's history—third baseman Brooks Robinson, shortstop Mark Belanger, and center fielder Paul Blair.

Like Joe McCarthy, Earl Weaver never played an inning in the major leagues; but, like McCarthy, Weaver went on to carve out for himself a place among baseball's most successful managers. In 1969 he won the first of three consecutive pennants, winning over 100 games each year, the first time that an American League club had achieved this since the 1929–1931 Philadelphia Athletics.

The short, colorful, umpire-baiting Weaver took over the team in mid-season 1968, guiding them to a second-place finish, 12 games behind Detroit. A year later his club finished 19 ahead of Detroit. In one season Earl Weaver's club had improved itself by 31 games over their chief divisional rival.

Baltimore's 19-game bulge over second-place Detroit was only one half game under the American League record established by the 1936 Yankees. On April 16 the Orioles took over first place and never relinquished it. By mid-July they led by 14 games, with a pitching staff that was insurance against a prolonged slump (only once during the pennant race did the team lose as many as four in a row).

Weaver's ace, Mike Cuellar, a veteran left-hander whom the club had obtained the previous winter in a trade with the Houston Astros, featured a screwball among his varied pitching repertory. Mike had had a rather nondescript career in the National League, which included stints with Cincinnati and St. Louis. In 1968 he was 8–11 with Houston. Arriving in Baltimore he became a new man, posting a 23–11 record and a 2.38 earned run average. Mike's fine ERA helped the staff lead the league in that department; this was the second of six consecutive years in which the Baltimore staff was to head up the league in this most telling pitching statistic. In trying to account for the dramatic transition in Cuellar, one might consider that in Houston he was pitching for a club that generally sat at the bottom in fielding; in Baltimore he found himself working for one of the best fielding teams ever. Particularly helpful for the left-handed Mike, who usually faced lineups stacked with right-handed hitters, was having Brooks Robinson and Mark Belanger covering the left side of his infield.

Weaver's second 20-game winner was another lefty, 26-year-old

Earl Weaver   Mike Cuellar

Mark Belanger
(Photo: J. J. Donnelly)

Brooks Robinson about to
get his man

Dave McNally. One of the many outstanding pitchers developed by the
Baltimore farm system, McNally started off the 1969 season like a man
with a mission. He won his first 15 decisions, not losing a game until
August 3. He finished up at 20–7, the second of four consecutive 20-
win seasons he put together from 1968 through 1971. He contributed
four shutouts to the staff's league-leading 20 (which tied them with
Detroit where Denny McLain pitched nine by himself).

The third big winner on the Baltimore staff in 1969 was 23-year-
old Jim Palmer, a tall, limber-armed right-hander who threw a rising
fastball and who was to become the greatest of Oriole pitchers and one
of the greatest of modern times. He joined the team in 1965 at the age
of 19. A year later he had become one of the aces, winning 15 games
and adding a shutout victory over the Dodgers in the World Series. The
following year he suffered from tendinitis of the arm and shoulder and
his career seemed to be over. He spent the better parts of the 1967 and
1968 seasons in the minor leagues. So dismal did his future look that
the Orioles left him exposed to the baseball draft in 1968, but no other
team would gamble a few thousand dollars on him.

Palmer rejoined the Orioles in 1969 and made a spectacular come-
back. Despite a back injury, which laid him up for nearly six weeks

during the season, he won 16 and lost 4 for a league-leading .800 winning percentage, pitched 6 shutouts and had a 2.34 earned run average, second lowest in the league.

Through the Orioles' three pennant-winning seasons of 1969, 1970, and 1971, Cuellar, McNally, and Palmer were 20-game winners eight times between them, with Palmer's 16-win total in 1969 their only miss. Cuellar's three-year record was 67–28, McNally's 65–21, Palmer's 56–23. These three sturdy Gibraltars constituted the core of one of the most consistently effective pitching staffs of the postwar era.

Weaver's fourth starter was chunky, 5'8" right-hander Tom Phoebus. The 27-year-old Phoebus was playing in his third full year with the Orioles and his last effective one. His record stood at 14–7. Tom, who had broken in with two straight shutouts in 1966 and pitched a no-hitter in 1968, tailed off after 1969; but in 1969 he was still strong, still a winner, albeit outshone by the three mighty hurlers ahead of him.

Supplementing his big four (they started 135 of the club's 162 games) Weaver had an exceptionally deep and talented bullpen, headed by righty Eddie Watt, who worked in 56 games, winning five and saving 16, with an earned run average of 1.65. Behind Eddie was lefty Pete Richert, 7–4 with 12 saves and a 2.21 ERA. Also in the Oriole pen was 38-year-old Dick Hall, a 6'6" veteran who had a 5–2 record with a 1.91 ERA. Dave Leonhard, another right-hander, was 7–4 with a 2.49

Dave McNally   Jim Palmer

Tom Phoebus

Eddie Watt

Pete Richert

Dick Hall

Andy Etchebarren

Brooks Robinson

ERA. Burly Marcelino Lopez, who was 5–3, rounded out Weaver's relief corps.

Weaver's regulars provided strong, multiple talents at virtually every position. They were durable too, no regular playing in fewer than 142 games, except for the catcher, where Earl platooned Elrod Hendricks and Andy Etchebarren.

The heart and soul of this team were the Robinsons, Brooks and Frank, two of the three sure Hall of Famers on the squad (Palmer being the other).

Brooks Robinson has gained the reputation of being the premier defensive third baseman in all of baseball, and since he was stationed at the bag for 23 years one assumes sufficient evidence has been compiled. Although not especially quick afoot, Robinson possessed astonishing reflexes. Going to his right or to his left, and, most spectacularly, coming in for a bunt or slow roller and making a swift scoop and underhanded throw off of one foot while almost parallel to the ground, he was as exciting and breathtaking to watch as a 500-foot home run.

In 1969 he won one of his 11 fielding titles at third base and one of his 8 most-assists titles (both league records). When early in his career Robinson was scheduled to be farmed out because of weak hitting, the Oriole pitchers went to the club's manager Paul Richards and begged

Frank Robinson

Boog Powell, 19-year-old first
baseman with the Rochester
Red Wings in 1961

Thunder over Baltimore. Left to right, Boog Powell,
Brooks Robinson, Frank Robinson

him not to do it. "They didn't care if he never got a hit," Richards said. "They wanted him in there."

In due time Brooks became a fine hitter, winning the Most Valuable Player Award in 1964 for his all-around play, which included a .317 batting average and a league-leading 118 runs batted in. In 1969, however, he had a decidedly uncharacteristic season at bat, hitting .234, a low figure but in Robinson's case a productive one—along with it came 23 home runs and 84 runs batted in.

The other Robinson was left fielder Frank, obtained from the Cincinnati Reds in 1965 in the most propitious trade the Orioles ever made. Robinson, probably the hardest hitter the Reds ever had, was only 30 years old at the time, but was considered by the Reds to be "an old thirty." Frank showed immediately that his dotage had been prematurely predicted, winning the Triple Crown and Most Valuable Player Award in his first season in the American League as he led the Orioles to the world championship.

In 1969 he was still slamming away, still one of baseball's most feared hitters. A man with natural instincts for leadership (in 1975 he became big league baseball's first black manager when appointed to head the Cleveland Indians), he was a driving, goading, inspirational force among his teammates. Leading by word and by example, Frank batted .308, hit 32 home runs, and drove in 100 runs.

As fine a season as Frank Robinson had, he was outgunned that

Dave Johnson   Reserve outfielder Merv Rettenmund

year by teammate John ("Boog") Powell, whom many believed deserved to be the league's MVP in 1969 (the distinction went to Minnesota's Harmon Killebrew). The massive Powell (6'4½", 240 pounds) had in 1969 the finest season of his 17-year big league career, batting .304, hitting 37 home runs, driving in 121 runs.

Another product of the fertile Baltimore farm system, Powell joined the club at the tail end of the 1961 season at the age of 20 and became a regular the following year. An impressive figure at the plate, Boog batted behind Frank Robinson, giving the Orioles a lethal right-left combination in the third and fourth spots in the lineup. Unlike many outsized power hitters, Boog pulled his considerable weight in the field as well as at the plate, committing only seven errors in his 144 games at first base.

Second baseman Dave Johnson was another nearly flawless glove in the Baltimore infield. When it came to turning the double play, the 26-year-old farm system graduate had no peer. Dave was one of the most consistent of the Orioles during their 1969–1971 pennant years, with batting averages of .280, .281, .282. In 1969 his 34 doubles placed him third in the league behind Tony Oliva and Reggie Jackson.

By the end of the 1980 season, the Orioles' 16-year-veteran short-stop Mark Belanger had compiled the highest fielding average of any shortstop in American League history—.977. If Luis Aparicio isn't the ace defensive shortstop in baseball's postwar era, then Mark Belanger is. (Interestingly, Belanger replaced Aparicio as the team's regular shortstop in 1968.) Sure-handed, strong-armed, remarkably quick and far-ranging, Belanger and Brooks Robinson virtually sealed off the left side of the Baltimore infield for nearly a decade. According to Detroit manager Mayo Smith, hitting a ball through the Baltimore infield "was like trying to throw a hamburger through a brick wall."

Normally a notoriously weak hitter, Belanger achieved his most successful year at bat in 1969 with an average of .287, one of Weaver's six .280-plus men in his starting lineup.

Like the 1961 Yankees, the 1953 Dodgers, and the 1942 Cardinals, most of the regulars on the superb 1969 Baltimore Orioles were home-grown products. Their talent-studded farm system allowed the Orioles to choose and select and build their team with just the desired weight and balance. Like Belanger, Brooks Robinson, Powell, Johnson, and many of the pitchers, center fielder Paul Blair joined the team after making the usual stops at Elmira and Rochester.

On a team of golden gloves, Blair stood out. No one—not DiMaggio or Mays—ever played a better center field. Impossible, game-saving catches were his trademark; no one was ever better at turning would-be doubles and triples into putouts (he led the league in 1969 with 407). Strong-armed, he tied for second among American League out-fielders in assists (fewer and fewer runners were willing to try his arm).

Paul Blair

Don Buford

Elrod Hendricks

Baltimore Stadium, home of the Orioles

Like many of his teammates on the 1969 club, Blair put together one of his most successful seasons in that banner Baltimore year. He batted .285, hit a career-high 26 home runs, and collected 178 hits, good enough to place him third in the league that year.

Weaver's right fielder and leadoff man Don Buford was acquired from the White Sox in 1968. A switch-hitter, the 32-year-old Buford was a fury of nonstop hustle concentrated in a muscular 5'7" frame. He was an outstanding leadoff man, particularly in 1969 when he batted .291, drew 96 walks, hit 11 home runs, 31 doubles, and scored 99 runs. A baseball and football star at Southern Cal, Buford had stolen as many as 51 bases for the White Sox. With the power of the Oriole lineup behind him, however, his base stealing was curtailed by Weaver, and Don had to be content with 19 thefts in 1969.

Weaver platooned catchers Elrod Hendricks and Andy Etchebarren throughout the season. Hendricks, drafted from the California organization in 1967, caught 87 games, batted .244, and hit 12 home runs. Etchebarren, another farm system graduate, hit .249. Hendricks flashed an almost flawless mitt that year, making just one error and leading American League catchers with a .998 fielding mark.

Considering the ingredients that must be blended in the creation of a truly great baseball team, one finds them in impressive abundance among the 1969 Baltimore Orioles. Their strong staff of starters and relievers, along the way to 109 victories, led the league in earned run average and shutouts; they also issued the fewest walks. Their hitting attack was balanced from top to bottom with power, speed, and average (Baltimore hitters struck out the least number of times of any club in the league). Defensively, few clubs had equaled them. That array of magical gloves made great pitching even better and made every Oriole run that much harder to match. Not surprisingly, they led the league in fielding with a .984 percentage—a fraction under the all-time record set by the 1980 Baltimore team—and made the fewest errors, 101.

.The Orioles went on to erase the Minnesota Twins in three straight championship series games to take the American League pennant. (They did the same thing to the Twins the next year and to Oakland in 1971.) Not even this mighty team, however, could unravel a miracle in the making. In the World Series that year they went down to defeat in five games to New York's "Miracle" Mets. The Mets, led by a dynamic mound duo of right-hander Tom Seaver and left-hander Jerry Koosman, proved many things that year, chief among them being that in a short series the best team does not always win.

CHAPTER 10

THE 1976 CINCINNATI REDS

In 1976 the Cincinnati Reds achieved a level of dominance so sweeping, so emphatic, and so definitive it has no parallel in the game's history. The Reds won 102 games in the regular season, finishing 10 ahead of the Los Angeles Dodgers in the National League's West Division, and thereafter did not lose again. In the Championship Series they stunned the Philadelphia Phillies by sweeping three straight games, taking the third game on the strength of a three-run rally in the bottom of the ninth. Moving on with supreme confidence, they swept the New York Yankees in four straight to win a world championship that had seemed all season long to be inevitably theirs.

This club, known as "The Big Red Machine," established total supremacy over its rivals as no other team ever has. In winning their second straight world championship, the 1976 Cincinnati Reds led not just the National League but *both* major leagues in the following categories: batting average, home runs, triples, doubles, hits, runs scored, runs batted in, total bases, slugging average, fewest errors, fielding percentage, and in addition led the National League in stolen bases. They had a spectacular combination of hitting, power hitting, speed, and defense.

The team glittered with talent, and 1976 was their year of culmination. They became the first National League team since the 1921–1922 New York Giants to win back-to-back world championships, after taking five division titles and four pennants in seven years, with Cincinnati players winning five Most Valuable Player Awards during those seven years.

Winning the MVP Award for the second consecutive year was

the club's dynamic 32-year-old second baseman Joe Morgan, one of the most lethal attack machines in the game. The 5'7" Morgan joined the Reds in 1972 in what was probably the best trade the Cincinnati club ever made. Along with Joe came pitcher Jack Billingham, infielder Denis Menke, and outfielders Cesar Geronimo and Ed Armbrister. To the Houston Astros went first baseman Lee May, second baseman Tommy Helms, and utility man Jim Stewart.

The fiery, multi-talented Morgan was a winner. Along with his box score talents at the plate, in the field, and on the bases, Joe brought the intangibles of leadership, excitement, and inspiration. In 1976 he had one of his best seasons. Possessing good power for a small man, he hit a career-high 27 home runs, batted .320, drove in 111 runs, scored 113, drew 114 walks, had a league-leading .576 slugging average, stole 60 bases, and fielded .981, second to Philadelphia's Dave Cash. On a team that placed seven men on the all-star team (five of them starters), Morgan was outstanding.

Leading the National League for the third year in a row in runs scored (130) and doubles (42), as well as in hits (215) for the sixth time, was the team's switch-hitting third baseman Pete Rose, one of

Joe Morgan
(Photo by J. J. Donnelly)

Pete Rose
(Photo by J. J. Donnelly)

Pete Rose scoring in his own inimitable style.

Pete Rose airborne again; but this one got by. (*Photo by Nancy Hogue*)

Johnny Bench
(*Photo by J. J. Donnelly*)

Johnny Bench one-handing it
(*Photo by Nancy Hogue*)

baseball's all-time models of excellence and consistency. The greatest 35-year-old baseball player extant, Rose batted .323 and led the league once more in desire and enthusiasm. He also led league third basemen afield with a .969 percentage. Three times previously he had been the league's top glove in the outfield; in 1980 he would win another fielding title as a first baseman. Sufficient evidence unto his versatility, also to his team spirit—how many superstars would willingly shift positions four times (he came up as a second baseman) for the good of the team?

Like Joe Morgan, Pete Rose's value to a team cannot be measured by statistics alone. His aforementioned desire and enthusiasm have proved infectious time and again (the testimony comes from team-mates). One of the few players in the game bold enough to set goals (200 hits per year and a .300 batting average), Pete is also one of the few players good enough to attain them. Once upon a time, in what now seems an era of economic deprivation, Rose stated that he wanted to be the first singles hitter to earn $100,000 a year. He achieved that, with yards to spare, at the same time becoming the first singles hitter to be a large-sized gate attraction, his nonstop hustle having become part of baseball legend.

It was a club of man-sized talents that stood out like the towers of an urban skyline, and none was more formidable than catcher Johnny Bench. By 1976 it was already apparent that the 28-year-old Bench, with the club since 1967, had established the credentials not just of a Hall of Fame career but perhaps as the greatest catcher in the game's history.

Bench's strengths were classic: power, the most feared throwing arm in baseball, and durability. In 1976 he was well on the way to tying the record for catchers by catching 100 or more games 13 years in a row. He was never better defensively that year, committing just two errors in 128 games behind the plate and leading National League catchers with a .997 fielding mark. Offensively, however, 1976 proved to be an off year for him. After four very strong years at the plate, Bench dropped to a .234 batting average, with 16 home runs but with a respectable 74 runs batted in. In the Reds' sweep of the Yankees in the World Series Johnny "atoned' with a .533 batting average, including two crushing home runs and five runs batted in in the fourth and final game.

In left field was 27-year-old George Foster, one of the game's most devastating power hitters. Foster was acquired from the San Francisco Giants in a May 1971 trade for shortstop Frank Duffy and a minor league pitcher, certainly one of the most lopsided transactions ever. In 1976 Foster broke out with his first big year, batting .306, hitting 29 home runs and driving in a league-leading 121 runs—the first of three consecutive RBI crowns for him, an achievement that put him among some of the game's Valhalla names. George also gave this remarkable team their third defensive leader (along with Rose and Bench), his .994 fielding average being the best among league outfielders.

Another big socker in this relentless lineup was one of baseball's most prolific RBI men—first baseman Atanasio Rigal ("Tony") Perez. For 11 years, between 1967 and 1977, Perez never failed to drive in 90 or more runs. Uncanny with men in scoring position—"inspired," some said—Perez kept base runners churning in 1976, driving in 91 runs, batting .260, hitting 19 home runs and 32 doubles (every regular in the lineup that year had over 20 two-base hits).

Like some of his teammates, Tony brought to the ball park along with his many obvious assets some invaluable intangibles. The likable, popular 34-year-old native Cuban was considered the "bridge" between the club's English- and Spanish-speaking players, an elder statesman who commanded the respect of all. Tony's trade to Montreal after the season was considered a serious mistake by many.

Cincinnati's 26-year-old right fielder Ken Griffey led the club in hitting in 1976 with a .336 batting average. The fleet-footed Griffey (he stole 34 bases), playing only his second full year in the big leagues, challenged for the batting crown down to the last day of the season, losing out to Chicago's Bill Madlock by three points. Batting ahead of

George Foster (*Photo by
J. J. Donnelly*)

Ken Griffey
(*Photo by Nancy Hogue*)

Tony Perez soon after being
traded to Montreal (*Photo by
J. J. Donnelly*)

Dan Driessen, hard-hitting
reserve first baseman (*Photo
by J. J. Donnelly*)

the busters in the Reds lineup, Ken, who pounded out 189 hits, scored 111 runs. Griffey was one of three Cincinnati players to score over 100 runs in 1976, a statistic worth mentioning because only two other players in the league scored over 100 times that year.

Like regulars Rose, Bench, Perez, and Griffey, shortstop Dave Concepcion was a product of the Cincinnati farm system. Dave joined the Reds in 1970; in 1971 and 1972 he batted all of .205 and .209. The Reds, enchanted by his glove, decided to stick with him, confident he would hit. He did. He moved his average up into the .280s and in 1976 weighed in with a .281 mark. By 1976 Concepcion had come into his own, an all-star shortstop for the second year in a row. Deft afield—he led the National League shortstops in putouts and assists in 1976—and with good speed afoot and a sharp line-drive bat, he helped give the Reds one of the strongest and best-balanced infields seen in the league in decades.

Cincinnati's fifth .300 hitter in its regular lineup was center fielder Cesar Geronimo, obtained from Houston in the Joe Morgan trade. Geronimo batted .307 in 1976, his best season ever. But the winged-footed 28-year-old's most notable contributions to the team were probably defensive. One of the game's fine old clichés was dusted off once more on behalf of the Reds' center fielder: "Two thirds of the earth's surface is covered by water; the other third is covered by Cesar Geronimo." Four

Dave Concepcion
(*Photo by J. J. Donnelly*)

Cesar Geronimo
(*Photo by J. J. Donnelly*)

Doug Flynn
(Courtesy Cincinnati Reds)

Bob Bailey
(Courtesy Cincinnati Reds)

years running, from 1974 to 1977, he was named as an outfielder on *The Sporting News* National League All-Star Fielding team. For a man with a glove as splendid as Geronimo's, a .307 batting average was a decided bonus.

Along with their powerful lineup of regulars, the Reds also had good bench strength in 1976. Utility infielder Doug Flynn batted .283 when he could break in, usually to spell Morgan or Rose. Outfielder Ed Armbrister batted .295 and veteran Bob Bailey .298. But with none of the regulars appearing in fewer than 135 games, it was a long season for the irregulars.

A weakness, if one existed on this great team, was a comparative one. The pitching was good, but none of Cincinnati's mound stars had the stature of a Rose or a Bench or a Morgan or a Foster. The Reds' staff was handled with consummate skill by Manager George ("Sparky") Anderson, a 42-year-old prematurely white-haired former infielder. Sparky had put in one season as a big league player with the Phillies in 1959, hitting a modest .218 before returning to the minor leagues. By 1964 he had begun his managing career with Toronto of the International League. The Reds hired him in 1970, and the former light-hitting infielder won the pennant in his first season.

Likable and easygoing, Anderson was popular with his players,

Sparky Anderson giving his side of the story
to the plate umpire (*Photo by Nancy Hogue*)

Gary Nolan

Don Gullett (*Photo by Nancy Hogue*)

though his quick trips to the mound earned him the name "Captain Hook." Sparky could be rather abrupt at lifting his pitcher, but it was hard to argue with success—five division titles, four pennants, and two world championships in his first seven years with the Reds. Like any good manager, Anderson worked the talent at hand, and at hand, particularly in 1976, was a strong and effective bullpen.

Arm injuries deprived the Reds of what might have been two of the 1970s' glittering hurling talents. Right-hander Gary Nolan joined the Reds in 1967, a 19-year-old with a burning fastball. He posted a 14–8 record in his rookie year, with 206 strikeouts. Arm miseries gradually wore the youngster down, causing him to miss the 1973 and 1974 seasons. He came back with 15–9 seasons in 1975 and 1976 before arm problems ended his career. In 1976 Nolan was the club's top winner. His once overwhelming speed gone, he pitched with great craft and guile, walking just 27 men in 239 innings.

Left-hander Don Gullett joined the club in 1970, also at the age of 19, and stardom was predicted for the strong youngster with the intimidating fastball. But the injury-prone Gullett could seldom put in a full season. When he was on his game, however, he was difficult to beat, four times giving the club a .700-plus winning percentage. He had a typical Don Gullett year in 1976—a shoulder injury limited him to 23 starts and a final 11–3 won-lost record.

Rookie right-hander Pat Zachry put up a 14–7 record and the best

Pat Zachry

earned run average among the starters, 2.74, fifth best in the league and good enough to earn him a tie with San Diego pitcher Butch Metzger for Rookie of the Year honors.

Anderson's starting rotation was rounded off by veteran lefty Fred Norman, obtained from San Diego in 1973, who was 12–7; right-hander Jack Billingham, 12–10; and another rookie, righty Santo Alcala, up from the Reds' seemingly inexhaustible farm system, who proved a pleasant surprise with an 11–4 record.

The pride of Anderson's hyperactive bullpen in 1976 was second-year man Rawley Eastwick, a 25-year-old right-hander with some jump on his fastball. Another product coughed up by the farm system (along with Nolan, Gullett, Zachry, and Alcala), where he had been trained as a relief specialist, Eastwick was immense that year. Appearing in 71 games, he posted an 11–5 record, a league-leading 26 saves, and a handsome 2.08 earned run average.

After Eastwick, the most frequently employed bullpen operative was the 30-year-old right-hander Pedro Borbon, since 1972 one of the mainstays of Anderson's relief corps. Put in the shade by Eastwick in 1976, Borbon turned in another solid year for the Reds, appearing in 69 games, showing a 4–3 record and eight saves.

Will McEnany, a 24-year-old lefty, slumped off from a fine 1975 season, dropping to a 2–6 record and but seven saves in 55 appearances. Will regrouped in time for the World Series, however, and

Fred Norman (*Photo by Nancy Hogue*)

Jack Billingham

Rawley Eastwick (*Photo by Nancy Hogue*)

Pedro Borbon

Will McEnany
(*Photo by Nancy Hogue*)

Santo Alcala
(*Courtesy Cincinnati Reds*)

pitched well, coming in to save Cincinnati victories in the third and fourth games.

In mid-season the Reds brought up right-hander Manny Sarmiento from their Indianapolis farm club. The youngster—he was just 20 years old—gave Anderson an excellent half-season, winning five and losing just one, with an impressive 2.05 earned run average.

A year later the cast of regulars remained largely unchanged, except for the absence of Perez. The pitching staff, however, underwent an almost complete turnover, an unusual occurrence for a world championship club. By the end of 1977 Nolan, Zachry, Gullett, Alcala, and Eastwick were gone and The Big Red Machine was beginning to sputter, though it was still strong enough to take another division title in 1979.

While running in high gear, this Cincinnati club was one of the most effective ever. With two sure Hall of Famers in the lineup—Rose and Bench—and two other strong contenders for enshrinement in Cooperstown—Morgan and Foster—the Reds were fielding a team that glowed and sparkled with talent. With a Tony Perez considered only the fifth most potent bat in the lineup, and a .300 hitter (Cesar Geronimo) batting seventh and a .280-hitting Dave Concepcion batting eighth, the team's lethal offense speaks for itself. Combined with good running speed and extraordinary defense to back up a deep if not overwhelming pitching staff, the 1976 Cincinnati Reds were legendary in their time, one of baseball's true unbeatables.

At third base for Cincinnati: Pete Rose (*Photo by Ron Modra*)

THE GREATEST OF ALL

Could the 1906 Cubs' pitching staff have stopped the 1927 Yankees? Could the 1942 Cardinals have outplayed the 1976 Reds? No doubt any of the teams discussed in this book could have given any other a bad time over the short or long haul.

Baseball legend has it that the '27 Yankees were the game's greatest team, for they prevailed as emphatically and dynamically as any team in history. Yet the 1976 Reds had superior players at at least four positions—catcher, second base, shortstop, third base—and possibly a fifth, left field. And as talented as the Reds were, they were inferior to the 1953 Dodgers at first base, center field, and right field, and were equally matched behind the plate and at shortstop.

Because they played in the dead ball era, the 1906 Cubs and 1911 Athletics were unable to pile up the dramatic long-ball records of other great teams. Nevertheless, Connie Mack always insisted his 1911 team was superior to his 1929–1931 club, a perennial contender for all-time honors. The latter club, however, was never overwhelmingly strong at second, short, or third; and outside of Jimmie Foxx, their infield could not compare to the infields of the 1936 Yankees, 1953 Dodgers, 1969 Orioles, or the 1976 Reds.

In searching for a perfect balance of hitting, speed, and defense, bettering the 1953 Dodgers, the 1969 Orioles, or 1976 Reds would be difficult. These clubs had everything in their lineups a manager could want. One suspects, though, that when certain intangibles like spirit and daring and determination are taken into account, the 1942 Cardinals might well have run any team in history off the field. This was a team that refused to be beaten. How they would have fared in a match-up with the awesome lineups of, say, the 1936 Yankees or 1961 Yankees, must be left to the realm of speculation.

No doubt the 1929–1931 Athletics could hit with the 1927 Yankees, or that the 1936 Yankees, 1953 Dodgers, 1961 Yankees, and 1976 Reds could hit with anybody. So the discussion of which was baseball's greatest team finally comes down to that most crucial aspect of the game—pitching. Of the teams on the present list, the 1906 Cubs had, statistically, the most outstanding pitching, even taking into consideration that they worked in an era of depressed earned run averages. Other strong pitching staffs show up on the 1911 Athletics, the 1942 Cardinals, and 1969 Orioles.

There is another set of pitchers, however, and they belong to the 1927 Yankees. Here this powerful team scores a distinct advantage over its strongest competitors. While several teams might match the 1927 club at the plate, and while several others can match their pitching, no club can offer the same strong combination of hitting and pitching.

When one thinks of the 1927 Yankees it is usually of Ruth and Gehrig, followed by Meusel, Combs, and Lazzeri. Overshadowed by that potent lumber parade is the pitching staff, one of the finest ever put together. Even with less offense, the '27 Yankees would still have won the pennant. The team averaged a little better than six runs per game, while their pitchers yielded a little over three. The staff of Waite Hoyt, Herb Pennock, Wilcy Moore, Urban Shocker, Dutch Ruether, and George Pipgras was not carried by the hitters. Among pitchers with 200 or more innings of work in that heavy-hitting season, there were only five in the league with earned run averages under 3.00, and three of them were on the Yankees—Hoyt, Moore, and Shocker (Pennock was at 3.00 exactly). The 1927 Yankees were one of the few teams to sweep not only most of the offensive titles in the league, but also to have their pitchers lead in earned run average, as well as shutouts.

For the best overall balance of pitching, hitting, defense, and running speed, one might have to select the 1969 Baltimore Orioles. For the best combination of power hitting, defense, and running speed, the '53 Dodgers and '76 Reds, with the Dodgers having the edge in home run power. With both clubs being fairly equal in pitching, one might say, arguably, that the 1953 Dodgers were the strongest team in National League history.

In selecting the greatest of all teams, however, one must bow again to legend and choose the 1927 New York Yankees in recognition of their awesome hitting, their depth of superb pitching, and their excellent defense. No other team quite matches this combination of outstanding talents.

INDEX

DiMaggio, Joe, 37, *70*, 71–76, *71*, *72*, 81, *84*, 100, 108, 120, 123, 131, 140
Dressen, Chuck, 103–17, *103*
Driessen, Dan, *149*
Duffy, Frank, 148
Dugan, Joe "Jumping Joe," *39*, 40
Durocher, Leo, 110–11, *110*
Durst, Cedric, *38*
Dykes, Jimmy, 57–59, *58*, 66–67

Earnshaw, George, *60*, 61–62, *63*, 67
Eastwick, Rawley, 154, *155*, 156
Ehmke, Howard, *64*
Erskine, Carl, 112–14, *113*
Etchebarren, Andy, 137, *137*, 142–43
Evers, Johnny, 1–5, *2*, 14

Feller, Bob, 50
Ferrell, Wes, 55
Fletcher, Art, *84*
Flynn, Doug, 151, *151*
Ford, Whitey, 128, *129*, 131
Foster, George, 148, *149*, 151, 156
Foxx, Jimmie, 50, 53–55, *54*, 66–67, 157
Frisch, Frank, *53*
Furillo, Carl, 103, 108–11, *109*, *110*

Gazella, Mike, *39*
Gehrig, Lou, 31–37, *33*, *34*, 47–48, *48*, 49–50, 55, 68–81, *69*, *71*, 123, 125, 131, 158
Gehringer, Charlie, 83
Geronimo, Cesar, 145, 150–51, *150*, 156
Gilliam, Jim, 103–8, 111–12, *111*
Glenn, Joe, *78*
Gomez, Lefty, 50, *80*, 81–83
Gomez, Ruben, 110
Gordon, Joe, 100-1
Goslin, Goose, 83
Grabowski, John, 40, *41*
Greenberg, Hank, 83
Gregg, Hal, 112
Gregg, Vean, 25
Griffey, Ken, 148–50, *149*

Grove, Robert Moses "Lefty," 10, 45–55, *51*, 62, 66–67
Gullett, Don, *152*, 153, 154, 156
Gumbert, Harry, *98*, 99, *100*

Haas, George "Mule," *60*, 61, 67
Hadley, Irving "Bump," *80*, 81
Hale, Sam, 57
Hall, Dick, 135, *136*
Hartsel, Topsy, *20*
Helms, Tommy, 145
Hendricks, Elrod, 137, *141*, 142–43
Herman, Billy, 86, 90
Hoag, Myril, 76
Hodges, Gil, 103–8, *106*
Hofman, Solly, *8*
Hopp, Johnny, 93, *94*
Hornsby, Rogers, 17
Houk, Ralph, 118–19, *119*, 128–31
Howard, Elston, 118, *124*, 125, 131
Hoyt, Waite "Schoolboy," *44*, 45–47, *65*, 158
Huggins, Miller, 40–47, *42*, *43*
Hughes, Jim, 114, *116*

Jack, Colby, 22–23
Jackson, Reggie, 140
Jennings, Hughie, 29
Johnson, Dave, *139*, 140
Johnson, Roy, 76
Johnson, Walter, 23, 50
Jordan, Tim, 6

Keeler, Wee Willie, 29
Keller, Charlie, 100–1
Kelley, Joe, 29
Killebrew, Harmon, 140
Klein, Chuck, 6
Kling, Johnny, 5, 7
Koenig, Mark, *39*, 40
Koosman, Jerry, 143
Koufax, Sandy, 50, 51
Krause, Harry, 26, 28
Krist, Howie, *98*, 99
Kubek, Tony, 118, 125–28, *126*
Kurowski, George "Whitey," 93, *93*, 101

Reniff, Hal, *130*
Rettenmund, Merv, *139*
Reulbach, Ed "Big Ed," 10, *11*
Richards, Paul, 125, 137–38
Richardson, Bobby, 118, 125, *126*
Richert, Pete, 135, *136*
Rickey, Branch, 85, 90, 103–17
Rizzuto, Phil, 100, 125
Roberts, Robin, 114
Robinson, Brooks, 112, 132–33, *134*,
    137–40, *137*, *138*
Robinson, Frank, 137–40, *138*
Robinson, Jackie, 103–5, *104*, 112
Robinson, Wilbert, 29
Roe, Preacher, 112–14, *115*
Rolfe, Red, 73, *74*
Rommel, Eddie, *64*
Rose, Pete, 145–51, *145*, *146*, 156, *156*
Ruether, Walter "Dutch," *46*, 47, 158
Ruffing, Charley "Red," 78, 79–83,
    100
Ruppert, Jacob, *84*
Ruth, Babe, 29–48, *30*, *31*, *43*, *48*, 49–
    50, 55, 68–71, 73, 121–23, 125, 131,
    158

Sanders, Ray, 93, *94*
Sarmiento, Manny, 156
Schoendienst, Red, 111
Schulte, Frank "Wildfire," 5–6, *8*
Seaver, Tom, 143
Selkirk, George "Twinkletoes," 73, *75*
Sheckard, Jimmy, 6
Sheldon, Rollie, 131
Shocker, Urban, 45–48, *46*, 158
Shores, Bill, *61*
Shuba, George, *109*
Simmons, Al "Bucketfoot Al," 50, 55,
    56, 66–67, 83
Skowron, Bill, 118, *123*, 124, 131
Slagle, Jimmy, 6

Slaughter, Enos "Country," 85–87, *88*,
    90, *91*, 95, 101
Smith, Mayo, 140
Snider, Duke, 103, 108, *109*, 112
Southworth, Billy, 86–87, *91*, 93
Spahn, Warren, 102, 125
Stafford, Bill, 131
Steinfeldt, Harry, 5, *6*
Stengel, Casey, 118–19, 128
Stewart, Jim, 145
Strunk, Amos, *20*

Taylor, Jack, 9–13, *12*
Terry, Ralph, 128–31, *129*
Thomas, Ira, 21, *27*, 40
Thomas, Myles, 47
Thompson, Don, *109*
Tinker, Joe, 1–5, *2*, 14
Triplett, Coaker, 95
Turley, Bob, *130*

Waddell, Rube, 42
Wade, Ben, 117
Wagner, Honus, 5
Walberg, George "Rube," 62, *63*
Walker, Dixie, *75*, 86, 95, 112
Walker, Gee, 83
Walker, Harry, 95, *95*
Walker, Rube, *107*
Walsh, Ed, 23
Waner, Lloyd, 48
Watt, Eddie, 135, *136*
Weaver, Earl, 132–43, *133*
White, Ernie, 99, *99*, 100, *100*
Williams, Dib, 57, *59*
Williams, Ted, 124
Willis, Vic, 10
Wilson, Hack, 66
Wood, Smokey Joe, 23
Wyatt, Whitlow, 86–87

Zachry, Pat, 153–54, *153*, 156